The Little Black Book
of
Maintenance Excellence

The Little Black Book
of
Maintenance Excellence

Daniel T. Daley, P.E., CMRP

INDUSTRIAL PRESS

Library of Congress Cataloging-in-Publication Data

Daley, Daniel T.
  Little black book of maintenance excellence /Daniel T. Daley.
      — 1st ed.
      p. cm.
  Includes bibliographical references.
  ISBN 978-0-8311-3374-0 (soft cover)
  1. Plant maintenance—Management. I. Title.
  TS192.D35 2008
  658.2'02—dc22

                                                    2008010929

Industrial Press, Inc.
989 Avenue of the Americas
New York, NY 10018

Sponsoring Editor: John Carleo
Copyeditor: Bob Green
Interior Text and Cover Design: Janet Romano

10   9   8   7   6   5   4   3   2   1

Dedication

To Lauren, Elizabeth, Jack and Liam, my grandchildren and
my sources of inspiration.

Also by Daniel T. Daley

The Little Black Book of Reliability Management
(Industrial Press, 2008) ISBN: 978-0-8311-33566

Contents

INTRODUCTION

Not long ago, I completed writing a book entitled "Little Black Book of Reliability Management". When I finished, I felt as though that book achieved its objective of providing a simple explanation of the variety of reliability tools that are available. My objective was to provide basic tools so that almost anyone could get started installing an effective reliability program. Not long after completing that book, I was reminded of one of the most basic rules of reliability. Simply stated, that rule is, "To get the results, you have to do the work".

That rule is a simple reminder that performing the analysis alone is not sufficient. After using Reliability Centered Maintenance (RCM) to identify the most cost-effective program for predictive and preventive maintenance, we still have two things we need to do:

1. We have to install the tasks that were identified (e.g. integrate those tasks into maintenance programs).
2. We have to actually perform the predictive and preventive tasks when they are scheduled.

The same is true of any of the other tools for improving reliability. They identify changes that are needed to improve reliability. Still, in order to achieve improvement, you must implement the recommendations.

All too frequently, we do the analysis but we do not perform the recommended work. There are a variety of reasons why the work does not get done but frequently ineffective or inefficient work management processes make implementation impossible. We simply cannot afford to do the work needed to become more reliable until we become more effective and efficient.

The mechanism that will help us become more effective and efficient is "Maintenance Excellence". Maintenance Excellence is the framework that fits over all the elements of reliability and maintenance to see they are aligned and complement one another. In addition to providing a comprehensive framework, Maintenance Excellence typically provides a detailed system for the work management processes, to ensure that the four distinct types of work are done in an effective and efficient manner. These types of work include:

- Routine or day-to-day maintenance
- Turnaround or overhaul maintenance
- Program Maintenance
- Projects

This book is intended to be a companion to The Little Black Book of Reliability Management. It is intended to ensure that tasks needed to improve reliability performance can be accomplished. Experience has shown that it is difficult (if not impossible) to achieve the best reliability without Maintenance Excellence and it is difficult (if not impossible) to achieve Maintenance Excellence without good reliability.

In addition to describing the various processes for

accomplishing work in an effective and efficient manner, this book describes how reliability is made an integral part of those processes through the actions of both maintenance personnel and operating personnel.

Some plants and some companies have chosen to spend hundreds of thousands of dollars installing the Maintenance Excellence practices described in this book. I am not so naïve as to believe that it is possible to simply read a book and everything will be better. This book is designed to provide a general description of the key elements of Maintenance Excellence so that they may be used as a basis for comparison.

By reading the book and then taking the time to assess the actual practices used in your plants or shops, you will understand the level of Maintenance Excellence in your facility. In some instances, companies will have spent a great amount of time and resources in the effort to implement Maintenance Excellence programs. In other instances, they will have spent none. The measure of how close you are to Maintenance Excellence is not related to the amount of money that has been spent. It is the product of many other factors and those factors are the subject of this book.

One last point is helpful in characterizing the objective of this book. In my experience there is a gap between knowing nothing about Maintenance Excellence and knowing a great deal about it. There seem to be a large number of people who know very little but have a strong sense that some improvements need to be made. They are a bit embarrassed to discuss those feelings because they do not know how to articulate their concerns and clarify their objectives. This group can include Plant Managers, and new reliability engineers. It can also include new Maintenance Managers. My references provide excellent detailed information on key maintenance processes, but they may take too much time for busy people. The references may also seem like diving into the "deep end of the pool". This book is intended to provide a "shallow end of the pool" so that readers can fill the gap between knowing a little and knowing a lot.

CHAPTER 1
DEFINING MAINTENANCE EXCELLENCE

The secret of joy in work is contained in one word - excellence. To know how to do something well is to enjoy it.

Pearl S. Buck

The term "Maintenance Excellence" has been around for a long time. Despite that, there is no place in the dictionary where you can look for a consistent meaning. Maintenance Excellence means different things to different people. While I will attempt to provide my definition, it is unlikely that many people will completely agree.

Universal agreement on a definition is not important. What is important is that you know what it means to you. It is also important that you and others working in the same plant or in the same company as you, have a consistent definition. Even more important than a consistent definition is a common vision of what things will look like when you arrive at maintenance excellence.

A number of years ago, I worked in one of the facilities that were part of a well-known U.S. company. To improve performance, this plant worked its way through an exercise called "Future State". The objective of the exercise was to streamline the organization, and while doing that, to install a variety of concepts currently viewed as part of "excellence" initiatives.

As part of the exercise:
- We formed teams
- We used forests of paper
- We talked until our brains ached
- We kept two facilitators employed full time
- We consumed a great amount of time

Despite all the time and effort, we did not develop a "common sense" of what the future state would look like. As it turned out, we worked for several years trying to achieve an objective for which there was little or no agreement. At the end of that time we simply agreed to say, "We have arrived. The future state is here. Let's get back to business."

The concept of "Maintenance Excellence" can contain a lot of the same vague altruistic concepts as "Future State". On the other hand, it doesn't have to. It is up to you. You can leave it vague and poorly defined or you can be very specific. In the following chapters, I will describe the specific business processes that I believe to be part of Maintenance Excellence. I will also try to describe some of the linkages with other systems and processes that are a part of Maintenance Excellence. But Maintenance Excellence is more than just systems and business processes.

At the beginning of the chapter I included a quote that I believe describes excellence. When you have excellence, you enjoy it. Not only you, but everyone in your plant or shop will enjoy it. That may seem unrealistic, but it is true. I have experienced it first hand.

A number of years ago, I was involved with an effort to upgrade the Routine Maintenance Process at a chemical plant. Prior to implementing the new process, every day was a new experience. Here are a few of the characteristics that describe the way maintenance was being performed:

- Every day was a surprise because the work for that day was decided at the start of the day.
- Operations personnel dictated the work that would be done without regard to the priority of the work order or level of preparation.
- Occasionally jobs would be started and stopped because materials or equipment needed to per form the work were not available.
- The plant was always short of resources and there were always arguments over who should get the resources that were available.
- Days were long. People came in early to get a jump start on all the changes in the day's schedule and they stayed late because work never seemed to finish on time.
- The maintenance budget and maintenance workforce seemed to always increase from prior periods. There was a constant belief that more was always needed.
- There was always a large backlog of incomplete work. Based on the size of the crew, the backlog was several months.

Rather than trying to describe the characteristics of the

new process here, I would rather say that we successfully completed installation of a new business process for handling routine maintenance. Since my company had a number of plants, after completion of this first plant I moved my attention to several other plants. About a year and a half after the routine maintenance process implementation mentioned above was complete, I started getting calls from first-line supervisors at that plant. Apparently, a string of problems hit the plant and the routine maintenance process suffered.

A barge broke loose on the Mississippi River and ran into the company's wharf causing a lot of damage. A severe electrical storm caused an outage that upset the plant in a way that required several days to recover. A major piece of equipment failed, causing another outage, and more emergency repairs. During these events, the plant moved from performing mainte-  nance in a well-planned and tightly-scheduled manner to being highly reactive. The duration of the problems disrupted the systems that were installed and allowed the individuals who prefer to work in a reactive mode to take over.

People were back to long days, fighting for resources, not completing all the needed work in a timely manner, and generally not enjoying work. The first line supervisors who called wanted me to return and get things back to the way they were when the routine maintenance process was working well. They wanted to get back to enjoying work. They wanted to get back to <u>excellence</u>.

You might be thinking that if excellence really existed in the first place, it should have survived the period of upsets and rebounded when things returned to normal. Maybe so, but I have seen a lot of plants drift away from excellence and I have yet to see a plant drift into excellence. There seems to be entropy associated with excellence. Properly functioning business processes consume energy. If you do not invest the energy needed to keep the process together, it will tend to disintegrate over time. There are always forces that tend to destroy the effectiveness of business processes. Some forces are well-meaning and some are intentionally disruptive. For instance, good people always want to make changes to "improve" the process. But if "improvements" are poorly documented, not everyone understands them. Or the systems have not been modified to support them, they will be more harmful than helpful.

> **Entropy: Entropy is the system for quantifying the measure of disorder in a system. The second law of thermodynamics states: In a closed system, the entropy will either remain constant or increase. The same is true in the business processes used by an organization. There is a tendency toward disorder and energy must be invested to maintain order.**

In the situation at the plant described above, we were

able to invest the right amount of energy needed to feed the entropy of the process and it returned to life. People were again enjoying their work and I stopped getting calls.

The fact that the routine maintenance process stopped functioning points out an important issue – no process stands alone. Certainly the processes associated with maintenance excellence do not stand alone. Take for instance the routine maintenance process in a chemical plant or refinery. The effectiveness of the routine maintenance process depends on cooperation from operations, engineering, purchasing and the safety department.

Functional Interface Diagram for Maintenance

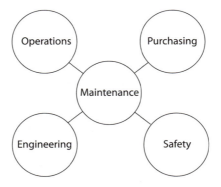

Maintenance both supports and is supported by a number of other organizations as portrayed in the diagram above. If Operations representatives choose to be disruptive and demand everything be done immediately, or out of the agreed order, any process will fail. If Safety chooses not to deliver permits in a timely manner, the process will collapse. If Purchasing does not stock the right materials or deliver them on time, the process will fail. If engineering has not built a reliable and maintainable facility, the Routine Maintenance Process (RMP) will struggle to stay ahead of failures. In fact, without a reasonable level of reliability, it is impossible to have Maintenance Excellence. (And without Maintenance Excellence, it is impossible to achieve the maximum level of reliability.)

On the other hand, in a situation where true Maintenance Excellence exists, everyone is more likely to enjoy their work.

- Purchasing does not spend all its time expediting orders.
- Safety personnel can plan their work better and be better prepared.
- Operations do not have to argue for resources to complete jobs that should have been done some time in the past.

Apart from making people "feel good", what other characteristics are a part of Maintenance Excellence?

Two separate but related characteristics of Maintenance Excellence are effectiveness and efficiency. Effectiveness is a measure of the ability to perform the intended function in a timely and complete manner. Efficiency is a measure of the ability to accomplish required objectives with the minimum expenditure of resources. It is possible to be effective without being efficient. It is possible to be frugal without being effective, but the concept of being efficient without being effective is a paradox.

Effectiveness: Effectiveness is a measure of the ability of an individual or an organization to complete the intended function in a timely and complete manner.

Efficiency: Efficiency is a measure of the ability of an individual or organization to complete the required objectives using the minimum amount of resources.

Throughout my career, I have encountered a small number of individuals with whom I shall always associate the concept of effectiveness. I recall a comment pertaining to one of these individuals, "You need to be absolutely certain you want something before asking him for it, because it is a certainty he will deliver it". I view the individuals in that small group as "hit men". When you give them a "contract" the job is as good as done.

Effective organizations are made up of "hit men". Their customer fills out a work order, they assign a needed-by date and they can be confident the work will be completed on time.

On the other hand, some hit men use a lot of bullets in completing their function. They use a lot more ammunition than was needed to complete the job. In the Maintenance Excellence business, our hit men need only one well-placed bullet and it need be of only a small caliber. Our hit men are both effective and efficient.

So an organization that exhibits Maintenance Excellence can be characterized as one that gets things done with the least amount of resources and smiles all the time while they are doing their job. Hmmmm. When the characteristic is described in that manner, it brings to mind the term "professional".

Maybe that would be a good way to describe Maintenance Excellence. It is a way of performing maintenance that appears to be very professional.

In all honesty, when I see most people performing maintenance, it doesn't appear very "professional" to me. If a function is being done in a "professional" manner, what are the characteristics I would use to describe it?

- Educated
- Articulate
- Caring
- Dedicated
- Highly skilled
- Competent
- Organized
- Clean

When I think of the term "professional" it brings to mind a

doctor's office. (Well maybe not). Or maybe it would be an attorney's office. (Definitely not!) The term "professional" does bring to mind the ability to cope with every obstacle in a thoughtful and organized manner. One would not picture a true professional in a situation where problems are allowed to linger unattended, or where the responses to important issues are late. True professionals treat people in a fair manner and with dignity. True professionals are able to manage most situations in a manner that seems to keep them above the fray, but they know when it is necessary that they get their hands dirty, and they do not hesitate to do so. True professionals tend to avoid situations in which they become flustered and are forced to act in an unprofessional manner.

Now picture everyone involved in your plant maintenance as being able to act in the manner described above. It requires thinking before acting and then acting in a professional manner.

Ask yourself, does your current system allow individuals to act in a professional manner or does it cause them to act in an unprofessional manner. Do people approach maintenance in a thoughtful, methodical manner, or is it part of the culture and a result of the environment to simply react in a stampede and continually struggle for resources.

Individuals may learn to survive in an unorganized, unstructured, and undisciplined system without obvious quarrels at every turn, but they may have settled into the appearance of cooperation because they recognize who has the power (not who is right), or because of apathy. Of all the measures I have ever seen, none of them compares the true priority of work being done to the true priority of the work that should have been done and was left undone. That measurement would tell whether power or influence is diverting resources:

- From where they should go.
- To the places where the biggest, or the loudest, or the most powerful individuals want them to go.

I recall an instance in which I was involved in installing a new Routine Maintenance Process at a particularly large plant. This plant was broken into approximately twenty separate and distinct operating areas, each with its own operating and maintenance function. The maintenance resources were shared across the entire plant, so a part of the problem facing the new RMP was the need to manage competing priorities and properly allocate available resources (craftsmen). In the past, it was common for the loudest or the most influential individuals to receive more resources than was justified by the priority of their work. Part of installing a successful RMP involved changing the culture and convincing the powerful and influential individuals to allow the system to work.

I recall the words of one of the most powerful and influential (and heretofore the most disruptive) individuals when he finally understood how he needed to act "I needed to learn how to get as big of a kick out of making the schedule work as I used to get out of trashing it every day". When this individual learned to act like a professional, he allowed the others around him also to act as professionals.

At the very root of "Maintenance Excellence" is the culture change needed to create a professional atmosphere for maintenance. But the path to achieve this culture change is not based on simply telling everyone to go out and "play nice". It is necessary to implement organized, structured, and disciplined systems that allow people to complete their work and do so while acting in a professional manner.

In maintenance, a variety of different forms of work is accomplished. Each and every form of work needs to be done in a professional manner to achieve "excellent" results. Different companies and different consultants choose to portray the building blocks in Maintenance Excellence in different ways. Some have a myriad of elements that form a pyramid leading to maintenance excellence. Others tend to focus on just a few items. There is probably no right way and no wrong way. The important thing is to address all the work being done and to recognize all the issues that affect that work.

In this book, I will describe four distinct work management processes. They differ in that they all tend to happen in a different time frame. In the second chapter, I will attempt to describe the importance of recognizing the time frame in which an individual is focusing his attention.

- The Routine Maintenance Process (RMP)
- The Turnaround Process (TAP)
- The Program Management Process (PMP)
- The Project Process (PJP)

In addition to the work management processes, there is the subject of reliability. It is impossible to achieve Maintenance Excellence without an adequate level of reliability, and it is impossible to achieve excellent reliability without some semblance of maintenance excellence.

There are several elements that are part of a comprehensive reliability process. Although this book is not intended to cover the subject of reliability, there are many books that do so (Including the Little Black Book of Reliability Management by this author). For the purposes of this discussion, I would like to confine my comments to aspects of reliability programs that tie directly back to Maintenance Excellence.

These subjects can be arranged under the following headings:

- The Reliability Process
- Reliability Centered Maintenance
- Predictive Maintenance
- Preventive Maintenance

In addition to the subjects described above, there are several other related subjects listed below, that play a part in Maintenance Excellence. Some comprehensive Maintenance Excellence programs tend to view these areas as separate and distinct elements. Others tend to view them as parts of the basic work management processes mentioned earlier. I will address these issues separately but try to show how they are closely integrated with the work management processes that form the basis of Maintenance Excellence.

- Precision Maintenance
- Total Productive Maintenance / Operator-Driven Reliability
- Key Performance Indicators

A final comment about Maintenance Excellence deals with how maintenance is viewed within your company and by its investors. I have worked in situations where maintenance was seen in a variety of ways. In many, maintenance was viewed as a necessary evil. In one unusual situation, there was a saying, "The refinery was built only to give the maintenance department something to keep it busy."

In situations where Maintenance Excellence exists, maintenance is seen as a "Profit Center". The maintenance function is viewed as the mechanism for finding the "hidden factory" or capacity that is being lost to poor reliability and poor availability. Companies with true Maintenance Excellence can maintain their facilities at less than half the cost of companies with poorly-managed maintenance.

Viewed in total, Maintenance Excellence is a "differentiator" and it provides a competitive edge for companies that have achieved it. Facilities that are reliable, and that have well-structured and well-disciplined work management processes, are much better equipped to deal with distractions and to seize opportunities. Maintenance is one of the most challenging aspects of any business. So that handling maintenance with excellence and professionalism makes it unacceptable for any other aspect of the business to be handled in a less than professional manner.

Maintenance Excellence sets the standard.

Additional Thoughts from References

Wireman, Terry; *World Class Maintenance Management;* Industrial Press, New York; 1990

> For additional thoughts on some of the subjects related to Maintenance Excellence, the reader is directed to this reference. In it, the author spends time focusing on the structure of maintenance organizations, roles of key staff members, and integration with other plant organizations..

Lamb, Richard G., *Availability Engineering & Management for Manufacturing Plant Performance*, Prentice-Hill Inc., New York, 1995

> Readers are referred to this text as a source that describes systems used to analyze maintenance performance as it is reflected in its products, reliability, and availability.

Senge, Peter M.; *The Fifth Discipline, The Art & Practice of the Learning Organization*; Doubleday Publishing; New York; 1990

Readers are directed to this text for many of the philosophies that are basic to Maintenance Excellence or to excellence in any organization or pursuit. Clearly the willingness and desire to be a "learning organization" is a basic aspect of excellence. For excellent organizations, understanding "why" is not discretionary, it is part of their very core.

CHAPTER 2
WHAT MAKES A WORK MANAGEMENT PROCESS WORK?

The leaders who work most effectively, it seems to me, never say "I." And that's not because they have trained themselves not to say "I." They don't think "I." They think "we"; they think "team." They understand that their job is to make the team function. They accept responsibility and don't sidestep it, but "we" gets the credit. This attitude is what creates trust, what enables the task to get done.

Peter Drucker

Every day, most of us participate in a business process or work management process of one kind or another. (In this context, I use the term "business process" to mean the structured steps and procedures used to conduct any generic business function. I use the term "Work Management Process" or "WMP" to refer specifically to a business process that is designed to manage the accomplishment of work.) In some instances, individual are involved at work and we are fully aware of the part they should play. In other instances, involvement is part of day-to-day life and we are simply the "civilians" involved in a process being operated by a business with which we interact. In any event, if our interaction is natural and intuitive, the process has been well designed and people are cooperating to allow it to work well.

Examples and Counter-Examples

As an example, let's think about the business process of buying and selling hamburgers. Most everyone has bought a hamburger from McDonalds so we are familiar with the process, at least from the viewpoint of the customer. The signs on the golden arches say that several billion hamburgers have been sold, so the process used to sell their hamburgers has been used a lot.

As you are probably aware, the process begins before the customer walks in the door. Preparations have been made and some kinds of food have been cooking in anticipation of your arrival. When you walk in the door, several features of the business process are apparent.

There are stanchions and chains that help people form orderly lines leading to the order takers and cash registers. There are also signs telling which cash registers are open and which are closed. There are large signs over the counter where order takers and cash registers are located, telling what products are for sale and what they cost.

As you pass through the line, you are expected to read the signs and decide what you want to order. An implicit expectation is that you will not order more than you can afford and that you will choose only products listed on the menus. When you finally get to the order taker, you describe your order and any special requirements you might have (e.g. no pickles). The order taker punches your order into the cash register and some magic begins to take place in the background. The cash register automatically sums up the total amount for your purchase and the order taker requests that amount. Once you offer a specific amount of currency, the order taker rings up that amount in the cash register and the cash register automatically calculates the proper change. The order taker returns the proper change and asks you to step aside while your order is being prepared so that the next customer can be served.

The magic that took place in the background involved the capabilities of the information system (connected to the cash register) to support the business process. Once your order was punched into the cash register:

- The cooks in the back were automatically directed to begin preparing the portions of your order that are not already available.
- The financial system added the value of that sale to the cash contained by that cash register so when the register is closed later that business day, the cash amounts can be reconciled.
- The logistics system is notified of the raw materials that were removed from inventory to fill the order (a hamburger patty, a bun, etc.) so that those supplies can be replenished.

Once the hamburger is ready, the order taker assembles all the items in a sack, adds napkins and condiments (if requested), and delivers them to you.

None of this is rocket science but there are a few important subtleties. One important point is that you cannot order Bacon, Lettuce and Tomato sandwich at McDonalds. If a customer were to ask for a BLT, he wouldn't get it. McDonalds does have the ingredients for a BLT, but the systems are not set up to deliver BLTs. There is no button on the cash register labeled BLT. There are no procedures or instructions for assembling a BLT product. There is no pricing system for a BLT, and no instructions in the information system software for replenishing inventory for ingredients used to assemble a BLT.

This subtlety may seem obvious, but it is frequently overlooked. On several occasions, I have seen situations where the Routine Maintenance Process (RMP) was asked to perform small projects or tasks that were not "maintenance". The RMP is designed to perform maintenance (e.g. put it back the way it was) not install modifications or changes. The RMP typically does not include the engineering resources needed to handle changes, so these requests tend to constipate the system. Everything then comes to a screeching halt.

When senior managers come along with "off-the-wall" requests, the "Can-Do" participants typically hesitate to tell them "that is not what we are designed to do". In these conditions, the systems struggle to cope with the requests. It is not a lack of desire or cooperation. It is the result of the fact that the work management process has not been designed to handle that type of work.

For the vast majority of customers, the McDonalds business process works well. They naturally fall into line, get their hamburger and fries and leave satisfied. The process is well designed and quite intuitive. Most people ask the process to do only what it is designed to do.

I recall an example of a process that was not well designed. The movie, The Blues Brothers, began with a scene of one of the brothers being released from prison. Two guards placed him in front of a cage where the prisoners' personal property was stored. The business process for releasing a prisoner included a step where their personal property was returned to them. In front of the counter where prisoners were expected to sign for their property, there was a solid line painted on the concrete floor. A sign on the cage stated – Do Not Cross the Line. In order to obtain his articles and sign the clipboard, the prisoner was forced to lean forward at about a forty-five degree angle. This was the only way he could reach the counter while keeping his feet behind the line. This process was not well designed.

It would be possible to spend pages describing good examples and bad examples of work management processes and business processes. Instead, I will attempt to focus on two issues:

- First, what are the elements of a work management process?
- Second, what are the characteristics of a work management process?

In answering those questions, I will attempt to describe instances where proper designs lead to an effective and efficient work-management process.

Clearly, a great many processes have been poorly designed or poorly implemented, or function with insufficient discipline to be successful. In the mid-1990s, many business processes and work management processes were going through an initiative called "re-engineering". This was an effort that looked at the products and objectives of a process and identified ways to produce equal or better results with less waste. Often this description was a misnomer because the processes being addressed were never "engineered" in the first place. Those processes grew more from habit than conscious intent. Individuals were given a task to complete and they did it in the best way they knew. When the same or a similar task came along, they did it in the same way. As time passed and more of the same kinds of tasks came along, the same approach was used over and over again until the approach first used became the accepted "process". When first used, the "inventors" of the process were simply trying to perform a task; they were not trying to create an effective or efficient process.

Elements of a Work Management Process

Elsewhere in this discussion, I have used the terms organized, well-structured, and disciplined, to describe effective work management processes. Reading between the lines you probably already realize that a Work Management Process provides a step-by-step description of how a specific kind of work is accomplished. Because different kinds of work are accomplished in different ways, the work management processes used will vary. But, one thing that should be consistent, independent of the kind of work being managed, is that the process provides the detail needed to organize and structure the work being done and to form a basis for discipline.

Description of Key Steps of the Process

Earlier, I used an example of the business process used by McDonald's restaurants. In a sense, the process described is a work management process as well as a business process because it describes the activities used in cooking and packaging the product. If you were to examine the complete work management process, it would not simply say. "Now cook the hamburger". That description might be adequate for part of the time, but for the other part of the time, the person performing the task would use some highly creative approach that would not meet the standards that McDonalds hopes to maintain. The comprehensive work management process should not only provide sufficient details to ensure that the desired results are accomplished, but also that important requirements are being met.

For the McDonalds restaurant, the "cooking" step will be defined in sufficient detail to ensure that every customer gets what they expect when they take their first bite.

Significant Details

Generally speaking, the work management process needs to address significant details concerning:

- Why
- What
- How
- Who
- When
- Where

If there is no reason for confusion concerning a specific attribute, it does not need to be highlighted. On the other hand, if there is some issue that is relevant, it should be addressed.

For instance, if the reason why you are taking a step can have impact on the results, the reason "why" should be included. An example in the Routine Maintenance Process is the step when the first-line-supervisor is asked to make the job line-up in a specific manner. He is asked to say something to the effect … "and I will be back in two hours to line up your next job". The reason for including this specific pattern as part of the line-up is to create an expectation of how long the job should take to complete without doing so in an abrasive or confrontational manner. The basic step of the work management process is to perform a job assignment and line-up. The reason for doing so goes beyond simply assigning a job. It includes creating certain expectations concerning the job, like "work safe". Without explaining "why", the subtlety would be missed.

The same kind of subtle but important requirement can be associated with each of the other descriptors (what, where, when, etc.)

An example of how a specific task must be done occurs in the daily meeting between the maintenance first-line-supervisor and the operations coordinator. This detail involves the agreement that they are expected to achieve concerning the work schedule for the next day. I have found that people often prefer to de-emphasize this daily meeting by making it informal. They say, "We see each other all day long, there is no reason for us to have a special scheduling meeting."

In situations where the daily face-to-face meeting is de-emphasized, there is a pattern of little commitment to the schedule. The purpose of the formal sit-down meeting is to formalize the "contract" between the participants for achieving the agreed schedule the next day. The maintenance first-line-supervisor agrees to have workforce, tools, materials, and parts at the work-site ready to perform the work at the agreed-upon time. The operations supervisor agrees to have the equipment ready to be worked, and to have safety and operating permits prepared if needed.

These are just a few examples, but every step of a work management process has to be thought out, documented, implemented, and continuously disciplined, to achieve the desired results.

Process Map

Another element of a comprehensive (and properly documented) work management process is a process map. The process map is simply a flow chart that shows each step of the process along with decision points, and the various possible alternatives that result from making various choices. Once the work management process is implemented, each and every item of work will make its way through the steps shown in the process map, resulting in the most effective and efficient handling. Rather than spending any additional time on this subject at this point in the book, I will defer to discussions on the specific forms of work management processes in later chapters.

One point I would like to emphasize at this time comes from having been involved in the development of numerous process maps. Rather than thinking about the "norm" or the "rule' that describes the flow of work when everything goes right, people like to show how smart they are by invoking numerous "war stories" of how things have gone wrong in the past. This digression will result in the process map being developed to handle all of those problems. As a result, the process being developed will be cumbersome and inefficient.

The process you develop should be defined for the "rule" rather that for all the "exceptions". Then the process will have to depend on the intelligence of your leaders to deal with abnormal situations.

Process Clock

One element of an effective work management process that is frequently ignored is the process clock. It is not uncommon for the work management process to ignore the "clock" that controls the people managing the steps of the process and the "clock" that controls the people performing the work.

As an example, let's think about work being performed on a typical eight hour "daylight" schedule.

A typical eight-hour shift is broken into four parts:
1. The first part runs from the start of the shift to the morning break...nominally two hours.
2. The second part runs from the end of the morning break to lunch...nominally two hours.
3. The third part runs from end of lunch to the start of the afternoon break...Another nominal two hours.
4. The fourth part runs from the end of the afternoon break to the end of the day...another nominal two hours.

Studies have shown that the first period can be the most effective period of the day. They also show that the second and third periods are less effective, but still provide substantial opportunity for accomplishing work. The fourth period has the lowest productivity of the four periods.

Think about how your plant complies with this pattern. It is not uncommon to have safety meetings and other business meetings at the start of the day. It is not uncommon to allow break-in work to upset the start of the day. In some plants the day's schedule is not established until the half hour or so before the start of work each morning, so individuals are scrambling around finding tools and materials instead of performing valuable work. (To a craftsman, standing in line for a tool is "work". He gets paid the same when we ask him to stand in line or when we ask him to perform a task that will have lasting value.)

An "intelligent" work management process will take advantage of the normal work pattern. Work needs to be ready to begin first thing each shift. Meetings should be scheduled for less productive periods. If an emergency job comes up over-night and it was not sufficiently important for the workforce to be called out immediately, the workforce should not be reassigned from assigned "first-start" tasks until after the morning break. All work should be allowed to start as was scheduled on the previous day so that the period of highest productivity can be harvested without interruption.

In general, the first three work periods should be carefully managed to achieve maximum productivity on work of high enduring value. The fourth period should be used for clean up, meetings, and set up for tomorrow (or the next shift) work.

I imagine some readers are thinking, "But you are wasting two hours from every day". In reality, most plants and shops are deriving between two and one-half and four and one-half productive hours from each individual each day. Rather than decreasing productivity, the approach described above will increase productivity in most situations.

Making the above schedule work depends on integrating

the work management process with the desired work schedule:

- A schedule for each day needs to be determined the previous day.
- Participants need to discipline themselves to adhere to "first-start" jobs.
- Participants need to discipline themselves to disallow "break-in jobs".
- Maintenance first-line-supervisors need to have work-force, tools, and materials for all "first-start" jobs ready each morning.
- Operations supervisors need to have equipment to be maintained and permits for all "first-start" jobs ready for each morning start.

In plants and shops that work two or three shifts each day, the same patterns exist on each shift with one exception. For plants working round-the-clock, the first work period on days is by far the period of highest productivity of the entire twenty-four hour period. Also, the fourth period of the graveyard shift is the period of lowest productivity for the entire twenty-four hour period. As a result, the fourth period on graveyard shift should be used to set things up for the first shift on days. This way you can use your period of lowest productivity to further lever-age the period of maximum productivity. (Occasionally leaders like to create competition among shifts by comparing productivity for each shift individually. This is a mistake in that it prevents using the period of lowest productivity on one shift from helping the period of higher productivity on the next shift. Measurements should help support the view of all three shifts being a single team trying to maximize production for the entire day.)

While this scheme may seem like simple work scheduling, much of the success has to do with the way your work management process is designed and applied. Within your work management process, the following characteristics will ultimately determine how well you will take advantage of available productivity from your workforce

- The timing of meetings
- The way you deal with emergency work
- The way operating crews deal with work preparation
- The way "teams" are defined
- The way success is measured

Accountability – Responsibility Matrix

Accountability:
The dictionary definition for "accountability" is "to be answerable for."

In the context of a work management process, an individual who is accountable for a task is the one and only person in the organization who has been identified as needing to ensure that step of the process is successfully accomplished. That individual is expected to view his areas of accountability based on the motto:
   "Don't do your best. Do whatever is required."

Responsibility:
The dictionary definition for "responsibility" is
"involving the ability or authority to act on one's
own".
In the context of a work management process, an
individual who is one of several who share respon-
sibility for a step of the process is expected to
freely contribute his time and talents to ensure that
the process step is accomplished in a successful
manner.
Unlike the individual who is accountable, responsi-
ble individuals should be viewed as being willing
and able to fulfill responsibilities unless they
inform the accountable individual to the contrary.

If they have not notified the accountable individual
of their inability to fulfill responsibilities, they need
to do so.

Another piece of the documentation needed to describe an effective work management process is the Accountability – Responsibility – Matrix (ARM). The ARM results from first understanding the concepts of account-ability and responsibility, then applying those concepts to your work management process and your organization. When properly executed, an ARM can identify both voids and redundancies in your organization.

A simplistic way to view the ARM is that each and every task done as part of a work management process, must be included in the ARM, or nobody will be assigned to perform it. Another important point is that only one person can be accountable for any one step in the process. If more than one person is identified as being accountable, then no one is truly accountable. (If for some reason the task is not properly executed, it would be possible for the multiple individuals with accountability to blame each other for the failure.) Any number of people can be identified as sharing in the responsibility for the success of a task, but only one person can be accountable.

When one person is accountable, he is the person who must ultimately see that the task is accomplished or suffer the consequences.

Another way to think of accountability is by considering the ways in which an individual might fulfill his accountabilities. They are:

- Control – Here, the individual has all the resources needed to complete the task reporting directly to him.
- Influence – Here, the individual must use personal skills or charisma to cause individuals not under his direct control to cooperate in achieving the desired results.
- Escalate – Here, control does not exist and influence has not been successful, so the accountable in dividual has to take the issue to a higher level in the organization to obtain the needed results.

In any situation, the role of the accountable individual is to ensure that the step of the process for which he is accountable is accomplished in the intended manner. Clear accountability and a clear understanding of who is accountable for each step is part of the path to effectiveness of a work management process.

Each step of every work management process will have several individuals who share responsibility for the success of that step. An example of this relationship is the roles involved in the construction of a building. The Project Manager is accountable, and the structural engineer is responsible. The Project Manager seldom has the skills needed to complete the structural design, so he depends on the help and cooperation of the structural engineer. On the other hand, if the building is behind schedule or over budget, the owner does not hold the structural engineer accountable. That will fall on the Project Manager.

Role Descriptions

In the earlier example of the process for purchasing and delivering a hamburger, you probably recognize some of the steps from having participated first hand as a customer. In that process, everything was organized in a manner that allowed the customer's role to be successfully completed without much knowledge or any training. But what if you were asked to be the order taker or the food preparer? Could you successfully complete either of these roles? This work is not rocket science and many people could work their way through the processes if there were only one or two "cooperative" customers. There would be more difficulty during a busy lunch time or if the customer chose to be difficult.

Even in this relatively simple example, the participants need to stay within the defined boundaries of the process. When things become rushed or begin to stray from the boundaries of the normal process, the manager will step in and help. The manager may help the person making French fries or in bagging the orders. In some instances, you probably have noticed that the flow remains well orchestrated, even when things are busy. At other times, the process gets backed up and it seems to take forever to get served.

So what makes things work so well in some instances and not in others? In those instances that work well, does everyone just instinctively know what they need to do? Is everyone just overwhelmingly cooperative?

For things to work well, everyone does need to want to make the process work. No process is perfect and the desire to be cooperative and to make things work is important. But, everyone also needs to know their role. Each and every participant in the work management process needs a written role description so that all the participants can know both their role and the roles of all the individuals with whom they interact. Everyone needs to know their role, and fulfill the requirements. Where possible, they need to behave in a manner that best allows others to perform their roles successfully. When roles are not being properly fulfilled, individuals need to be coached or counseled to address shortcomings.

Role descriptions may not describe every step that every participant takes. But they need to describe every step that is important to achieving the objectives of the process. If any way of performing an act will work, the role description should allow flexibility. If there is only one way a task should be done, the role description should describe the requirements.

Integration with Information Systems

Most current work manage-
ment processes are supported
by some form of information
management system. The
system supporting the Routine
Maintenance Process is typically referred to as a
Computerized Maintenance
Management System (CMMS).

The Turnaround Process and Project Process are typically supported by some form of scheduling program that
incorporates a Critical Path Planning (CPM) algorithm
with workforce leveling capabilities.

An unfortunate note is that many of these information
systems are poorly integrated with the processes they
support and they are used in an undisciplined manner. In
some systems there is no clear requirement to collect
needed data or no requirement to collect it in a manner
that will make it useful. Sometimes it is left to the discre-
tion of the user how or if the system will be used. These
systems are expensive to purchase and maintain, and
when improperly used, they do not provide the return-on-
investment used to justify the expenditure.

As with other elements of an effective work management process, the manner in which the integrated information management system is used must be clearly defined and disciplined.

Some systems, like those that are part of SAP® suite of products, treat each step as an individual transaction. To move to the next step, it is necessary to properly complete the transaction. This simple feature causes the necessary information to be properly and completely entered. This feature will ensure that Key Performance Indicators and other information will be available when desired. Although other products provide greater flexibility in their use, if not tightly disciplined there will be no assurance that information will be available when needed.

Characteristics of a Work Management Process

In prior sections of this chapter, I have described the tools that are part of creating the structure for an effective Work Management Process. In the following section, I want to describe some characteristics that I believe are important to achieve as a part of implementing a WMP. The reason for discussing these points is that on occasion, I have observed them to have been totally missed. This omission reduced the effectiveness of the WMP.

Adapt Individual's Schedules to WMP

One reason why the work management processes that tend to develop naturally over time fail is that they require cooperation and, at times, people choose not to cooperate. All work management processes are based on a number of individuals performing their roles both individually and as members of teams. If the tasks that can only be completed properly in a team setting are not done well, the work process will not function as well as possible.

Let's use the Routine Maintenance Process as an example. In a large work setting, there are typically two instances where participants must function as teams. In one, the maintenance first-line-supervisor and the individual representing the operating function must meet and agree on the work that will be done tomorrow. Coming out of that meeting, both of those individuals need to be committed to do whatever is necessary to complete the agreed schedule. To be prepared for that meeting, both individuals have some preparations that need to be completed earlier in the day. If for instance, the maintenance person does not have a list of all work that has been planned, and has all material ready, he would be unable to describe all the candidates for scheduling. If the operations person does not know what equipment will be available tomorrow, he will be unable to determine what jobs should be scheduled.

If these individuals are to meet at a specific time each day it will be necessary for them to keep their schedules clear during that time.

As mentioned earlier, some WMP's do not work

because people choose not to cooperate. They do not make the effort necessary to perform tasks in a timely manner to be ready for the scheduling meeting and to keep the time of the meeting clear so that they can attend. When implementing a WMP, the concept of voluntary cooperation is not an issue. Conformance is not voluntary. The process is designed to require specific tasks and specific meetings to be done during specific times each day. Once the process design is complete, participants receive coaching (and counseling) to help adapt their own skills and schedules to the demands of the process.

Integrated with Customer Requirements

Let's return to the example of purchasing a hamburger from McDonalds as a typical business process. In this example, it is clear that the business process is designed to integrate well with the Customer Requirements. In fact, it is almost taken for granted that the business process will integrate well with the customers' needs.

In some ways this statement is true, and in some ways it is not. Several years ago I found out I am a Type II diabetic. That condition introduces a whole new set of requirements for diet, exercise, and health maintenance. Few restaurants offer menus that are truly integrated with the specific needs of the diabetic customer. Fortunately, diabetics are in the minority so the business processes (and products) are integrated with the needs of most customers. Or are they?

In the United States, there is a growing epidemic of obesity. This is not a situation like diabetes's that affects a minority of the population. It can affect the entire population. Again, few restaurants offer a menu that really serves the "needs" of a population at risk for obesity. Restaurants are successful because they provide what their customer "demand" rather than what they "need".

When viewing the subject of Maintenance Excellence, a maintenance organization that provides what their customer "demands" is a "reactive" organization. A maintenance organization that provides what its customer "needs" is a "responsive" organization. The ability to be "responsive" while being effective and efficient is significantly different from being "reactive". Like the example of the restaurant menu, the ability to transition requires the participation of the customer. In the restaurant example, the customer has to be willing to cooperate by purchasing the items from the menu that are aimed at "eating healthy". In a work management process, the customer needs to participate in the process in a manner that facilitates "responsiveness" rather than "reactivity".

For instance, the customer "needs" reliable equipment. Reliable equipment depends on completing predictive and preventive tasks when scheduled. Sometimes this approach may introduce some discomfort or added risks, as when one of a redundant set of pumps is taken out of service to perform PM. The customer may need to be educated to make him an intelligent and cooperative participant in the process.

In the end, the objective is to fulfill the customers "needs" rather than his "wants".

Integrated with Support Functions

Another characterization of an effective Work Management Process is that it is integrated with support functions. A significant portion of the return from investing resources needed to install and maintain an effective WMP, results from efficiencies that are available from support functions.

For example, one of the primary functions that support maintenance is the purchasing or supply department. In most plants, the supply organizations say that, "Maintenance is our largest customer." In some instances they even say, "Maintenance is our Best customer", but that is less common.

For the sake of discussion, let's explore the characteristics that makes maintenance a "bad" customer, then discuss how an effective WMP can turn that around.

1. Late scheduling results in lots of expediting effort and cost.
2. Poor planning results in expediting effort and cost as well as larger warehouses and inventory.
3. More reactive maintenance instead of proactive maintenance means more expediting, larger warehouses and inventories, and an inability to schedule tasks far in advance. These conditions create the need to keep more parts in inventory (rather than ordering them after the job is

scheduled).
4. More reactive work means more breakdowns, and therefore more costly replacement parts.
5. Less knowledge about consumption rates and less ability to forecast needs means less ability to negotiate prices.

When the maintenance organization has all the characteristics of a bad customer, the supply department will have all the characteristics of a poor purchasing function:

- Lots of expediting effort
- Lots of expediting shipping costs
- Large warehouses
- Large inventories
- Inability to negotiate price or volume.

Now how does an improved WMP allow the purchasing function to be better?

1. More proactive maintenance means less expensive parts.
2. More proactive maintenance allows for delivery of PM parts shortly before they are needed.
3. More proactive maintenance allows long term forecasting of need, allowing for price negotiation and normal deliveries.
4. Detailed planning means fewer parts are missed and require less expediting.
5. Longer term scheduling reduces sizes of inventories and the effort and cost of expediting.
6. Longer term planning and scheduling allows for the combining of inventories for multiple facilities,

resulting in smaller warehouses and smaller inventories (while still preventing added risk by maintaining proper insurance inventories).

Generally speaking, Maintenance Excellence is necessary to achieve Purchasing Excellence. The same is true of every other organization that supports maintenance and depends on their organizational excellence.

Organization Used To Lean-Out Activities and Resource Needs

In the last few years "Lean" and "Lean-Six-Sigma" have gained increasing popularity. In many companies these tools are being used to gain short term improvement. Unlike efforts that address an entire work management process, many lean efforts address only a troublesome portion of a process. A problem with taking this approach is that it is possible to make the troublesome elements look better at the expense of the surrounding steps of the process.

A common example of one function being "leaned out" at the expense of another function is the area of expediting. I have seen a number of examples where a purchasing organization has installed a few relatively insignificant tools that were intended to replace expediting without addressing the root causes for expediting in the WMP. After installing these tools, they eliminated the expediter jobs. Because the weaknesses in the WMP that caused the need for expediting were not addressed, materials still had to be expedited to keep the plant running. However, the Purchasing origination no longer had expeditors. So planners, schedulers, or first-line-supervisors in the maintenance organization had to perform expediting to keep work on schedule.

It has been my experience that "leaning out" pieces of a process is not effective over the long haul. It is better to view the process as a whole and not only a specific business process but those processes that support it and are being supported by it. It does no good to eliminate a resource from one organization only to have continuing need for that resource appear in another place.

When a comprehensive understanding of a work management process is developed, true efficiencies can be identified. It may be possible to reduce resources when one understands which tasks are being done that add little or no value to the end product or directly result in waste. On the other hand, there are occasions when one organization performs a task that does not appear to add value unless it is viewed from an overall perspective.

Discipline

Another characteristic of an effective WMP is discipline. By this, I do not mean to infer rigidity or friction, or any particularly negative connotation. I simply mean that people follow procedures in a consistent manner. Rather than adding rigidity, a disciplined approach often allows all participants to participate in a more relaxed manner.

There is less effort if everyone comes to meetings on time, knows the agenda, and is ready to participate. Individuals can be more relaxed if there is a clear understanding of what is expected, of them and of others. It is far less of a struggle for individuals new to positions or temporarily back-filling positions if they know what is expected and if others, who also know what is expected, can help newcomers slide into the groove.

Discipline is a "bad thing" only for individuals who want to do things "their way" and their way is inconsistent with what is required.

Evergreen

While it may seem that effective WMP's are pretty fixed and inflexible, the best are viewed as evergreen.

One reason why many WMP's become ineffective is that people want to make "improvements". The "improvements" they want may or may not result in improved effectiveness or efficiency, but they are always someone's "pet project". If you ignore the fact that there are always people wanting changes, the changes will occur "underground". Underground changes are not documented, people are not trained to deal with them, and systems and support organizations are not modified to align with them. As a result they create inefficiency and misalignment.

It is far better to be receptive of change. If anyone has an idea they should bring it forward. They need to continue using the process as it was designed until the change has been formally implemented, but all should be considered. If there is a value in making the change, and if all the participants are supportive, the change to the process is made. Process documentation is updated. Role descriptions are modified. Training is conducted.

In the end, changes are good. They keep people aware of the process, both the changed elements and the elements that remain unchanged.

Mechanism for feeding ENTROPY

Entropy is the quantified measure of disorder in a system. The concept comes out of thermodynamics. Instead of talking about it in absolute terms, scientists generally talk about the change in entropy of a system.

The second law of thermodynamics is: In a closed system the entropy of a system will either remain constant or increase.

This rule does not mean that systems necessarily must remain constant or become less orderly over time. It simply means that for all energy moving the system toward disorder, it is necessary to invest an equal or greater amount of energy resisting or restoring order.

In terms of work management processes, this rule means that, when someone decides they are going to make an "improvement" without the appropriate oversight and protocols, someone else is empowered to stop the change and be sure it is done properly.

Another example is the situation where people start ignoring procedures. Say there has been an emergency and people believe there is no time for planning. An effective WMP will contain an internal mechanism for policing these situations to make sure that order is maintained.

Some systems are built to be self regulatory. (For instance try to order a BLT at a McDonalds and see what you get.) But, in most systems, the situations leading to disorder are not as recognizable and not as easily corrected. Most WMP's need to have a number of people involved who "know what is right" and are not afraid to take corrective action when they see a problem.

Additional Thoughts from References

Conner, Daryl R., *Managing at the Speed of Change,* Villard Books, New York, 1992

> Those who have been through the daunting task of modifying a business process or work management process understand the pains of change that accompany that activity. Part of making a work process function as it was intended, is managing the necessary changes. Managing change can best be described as taking the steps needed to build the resiliency and acceptance of the individuals who are directly involved in the process. This text is an excellent source for addressing this aspect of achieving Maintenance Excellence.

Senge, Peter M.; *The Fifth Discipline, The Art & Practice of the Learning Organization*; Doubleday Publishing; New York; 1990

Effective work management processes are a key component of Maintenance Excellence. In addition to acceptance of change, it is important that the work management processes have the ability to learn and grow built into them. Any process that is static will become dated and archaic. This reference will provide the reader with some thoughts on how to integrate learning and continuous improvement based on that learning into the basic fabric of the work- management processes.

CHAPTER 3
OPERATING IN DIFFERENT TIME FRAMES

Effective leadership is putting first things first. Effective management is discipline, carrying it out.

Stephen Covey

Sometime ago I heard someone describe an effective CEO as a person who was able to see the future that will exist in twenty years. Clearly, if the leader can see the future, the company can be successful. Or can it?

For a moment assume that the CEO is a visionary who knows what will exist twenty years in the future. Now assume that everyone but the CEO is focused only on today. There would be little or no benefit to the CEO's vision. For there to be a benefit, each level of the organization would need to be translating the vision into tangible plans for successively closer intervals of time. Senior executives would need to lead changes required for the ten- to twenty-year time frame. The middle level manager would need to be leading changes required for success in the ten-year time frame. And so on and so on, down through the organization. If senior executives are micro-managing today's activities, then who is worrying about tomorrow? It is impossible for a person's mind to be focused on today and tomorrow at the same time. Tomorrow will always suffer because of the urgent issues needing to be addressed today.

The same kinds of problems exist in most plants. If you assign the person responsible for managing day-to-day issues with responsibility for long-term activities, like implementing projects, the long-term actions will never get done. The urgent current issue will always overwhelm the important long-term issues.

In the area of Maintenance Excellence, there are a number of time-frames in which individuals are asked to operate.

- Day-to-day or Routine Maintenance
- Turn around or Overhaul Maintenance
- Program Maintenance
- Project Maintenance

It is possible to discuss the importance of "time-frame" using these four categories, but it might be more helpful to do so in a different way. For the sake of discussion, let's use the following categories:

- Current Focus-Do it Now
- Day to Week
- Week to Month
- Month to Year
- Several Years

Starting with current focus or the "Do-it-Now" mentality, I can recall a situation (while in the Air Force) when one of my supervisors assembled an "idea-generation" meeting intended to gather ideas from people at all levels of the organization. When directly asked for his thoughts on a specific subject, one of the members of the hourly workforce responded by using one hand to indicate the level of his neck and saying, "You pay me to function from here down." Although the response surprised my supervisor and resulted in some laughter, management realized that it accurately portrayed the feelings of that person and quite a few others in the workforce.

What the person was saying was that although he wanted to do his job he was not interested in accepting a lot of the worries associated with being a manager. When he left work for the day, all his thoughts were on his family and his non-work-related life.

Organizational psychologists may dispute it, but a large portion of the workforce feels that way. They want to do their job and let someone else worry about managing things. These people are perfectly capable of performing jobs with a current focus but they will not be effective if asked to take on responsibilities for longer term issues. That's not an indictment of their work ethic; it is a simple recognition that they know their own priorities. Some people choose to apply long-term thinking to their family or community rather than their work place.

I recall an individual working for a large company who had an absentee rate of 20%. When he spoke to the man, his supervisor wanted to use terms that explicitly described the problem. After finding out that the individual used the time away from work to go fishing the supervisor asked, "Your record is just like being off one day every week. Why do you come to work only four days every week?" The employee responded, "Because I can't make it on three days a week." This individual knew his priority was fishing. He was not the kind of person who could be entrusted with long-term issues.

The above example is probably an extreme case, but there are more people who feel this way than openly admit it. Placing these individuals in positions that require a long-term focus is a mistake. They are not interested in either handling the responsibility or maintaining the focus.

In addition to the desire of some people to limit their focus to near-term requirements, there is sometimes an organizational <u>need</u> to do so. Some facilities have a significant amount of work that needs to be addressed on a near-term basis. The work might include fixing un-spared equipment, calibrating critical instruments, or other "do-it-now" (DIN) tasks.

In situations where there is a significant amount of "do-it-now" work to be done, it is best to separate the DIN Crew from the workforce for which work has been planned and scheduled. Past studies have shown that unplanned and unscheduled work can consume as much as four times the amount of resources as is needed for the same work if it is thoroughly planned and tightly scheduled.

As a result, it is best to keep planned and scheduled work from being interrupted by emergency work. Even a small number of interruptions or "break-in" jobs can devastate a schedule and result in significant losses in productivity. It is better to "sacrifice" the effectiveness and efficiency of a small number of people by creating a "do-it-now" crew than allow interruptions to contaminate your entire workforce.

The group of craftsman working on routine maintenance, their first line supervisor, and the other individuals responsible for providing liaison between other departments and the routine maintenance activity, constitutes the group working in the "day-to-week" time frame. The vast majority of routine maintenance is not DIN maintenance. At the minimum, there should be, scheduled for tomorrow. Better yet, routine work should be scheduled for a week or more in the future. Members of the work force should receive their assignments for the following day on the preceding afternoon.   First-line supervisors should be aware of the schedule for the entire week and use that entire period to collect tools and materials and stage the jobs. More will be said later about scheduling in the Routine Maintenance Process.

Small outages, some program work, and small projects, typically fall in the week-to-month time frame. Each of these items has specific reasons why they need to be well prepared and be executed properly when scheduled:

- For small turnarounds, vital equipment will be taken out of service, thus reducing plant thru-put.
- For unusually large programs and projects, crews or contract crews will be brought in at added expense.
- During outages, programs and projects, the kind of work being done is work that is not done every day. Frequently, it is not simple maintenance (put it back the way it currently is). Special work needs special preparation.

If this kind of work is managed by the same individuals responsible for day-to-week work, the near term responsibilities are likely to take precedent if there is a conflict. Thus, it is best to separate week-to–month responsibilities from both day-to-week work and Do-It-Now work.

Several different kinds of work fall into the category of month-to-year work. Moderate- to larger-sized turnarounds, moderate-sized projectsm and many plant or shop programs fall into this category.

As an example, let's discuss a plant painting program. Let's assume that the painting program is well-organized and has been properly funded for a number of years. For the sake of discussion, let's assume that the environment is such that a painting system can survive for seven years when the surface being protected has been properly prepared and the coating system is high-quality and properly applied. In these conditions, the entire facility would be broken down into seven areas, each representing nominally an equal amount of work, for the painting program. Each of the seven areas would be sequentially addressed during the seven-year cycle.

The typical work for the individual managing the paint program would include:

- Preparing a scope-of-work for the up-coming year.
- Bidding the work and letting the contract.
- Coordinating the work with managers of areas where work will be done.
- Preparing support (scaffolding, insulation removal, etc) for the area being addressed.

An example of coordinating work in areas being painted may involve preparing personnel in that area for the inconvenience that comes with the paint program being in their area. For instance they will need to put up with scaffolding creating obstacles. They may also need to cover motor air-cooling intakes and pump seals if abrasive blasting is anticipated.

In addition to the normal activities for keeping the program on schedule, the person managing the paint program should manage the "giraffe-program". In other words, he will manage the program for identifying and repairing the small spots where the painting system has been damaged or has failed ahead of schedule.

The point is that if the person being asked to manage the paint program is also asked to manage day-to-day activities, the intricacies of the paint program will be ignored.

The paint program is just one of many month-to-year activities that require dedicated attention if the work is to be done properly. A variety of inspection programs fall into that category as well.

An important point is that although there are individuals who love dealing with urgent problems on a minute-to-minute basis but choose not to be bothered with long-term responsibilities, there are also people who are very good at long-term organization. They thrive in settings where they can "plan their work" and "work their plan."

Finally there are activities in every organization that need to look several years out into the future. This long-sightedness may be the least well handled by all organizations. There are probably several reasons why it is poorly managed:

1. Current demands are clearly defined. Future demands are no so clear. People like clarity.
2. Fewer people have any "visionary" capabilities so they do not know what to do to address future needs.
3. Senior managers micro-manage in a current time frame. So no one beneath them in the organization can manage any further out in the future than their boss.

The last of the three is by far the most insidious. Senior managers that start each day with a meeting that focuses on "what went wrong yesterday" are performance killers. They manage by means of visions obtained from a "rear view mirror." No one beneath them in their organization can spend their time looking into the future because of the demand to "get tactical."

It should be clear that current technology provides us with the capability to build and maintain systems that will last ten years or more between failures. This knowledge tells us that to continue making progress we need to have someone thinking well out into the future. If our current equipment will last ten years, are there systems and components that will last fifteen or twenty years? If there are, can we afford them?

If you are focusing on yesterday, you will never know.

Additional Thoughts from References

Conner, Daryl R., Managing at the Speed of Change, Villard Books, New York, 1992

> I recall an old saying, "When Leaders do not lead, followers will not follow". I think what this saying tells us is that, when leaders do not focus on the future and prepare their organizations for the future, the followers will feel as though the future is being thrust upon them, and they will resist the changes that the future brings. On the other hand, when leaders are focusing their attentions several years out into the future rather than "managing using the rear view mirror", their organizations will know what is coming in the future and have more time to prepare. This reference describes the importance of the element of time in the process of accepting change in a productive manner.

Lamb, Richard G., *Availability Engineering & Management for Manufacturing Plant Performance*, Prentice-Hill Inc., New York, 1995

> Chapter 13 of the referenced text provides useful descriptions of several of the time frames in which key maintenance functions are accomplished.

Senge, Peter M.; *The Fifth Discipline, The Art & Practice of the Learning Organization*; Doubleday Publishing; New York; 1990

> In chapter 4 of this book the author introduces "the

laws of the fifth discipline". Several of these laws describe the relationship between time and learning, change, and organizational effectiveness. One is "Faster is slower". It again reminds us that change takes time and leaders need to be ahead of the people they lead (in time) so that change seems metered and timely to those being led. Another is that "Cause and effect are not closely related in time and space". This law reminds us that to have a nice shade tree to enjoy during our retirement, we need to plant a seed while we are still young. Similarly, for companies to be prepared for survival, they need to prepare for the future now.

CHAPTER 4
THE ROUTINE MAINTENANCE PROCESS (RMP)

Management means, in the last analysis, the substitution of thought for brawn and muscle, of knowledge for folkways and superstition, and of cooperation for force. It means the substitution of responsibility for obedience to rank, and of authority of performance for the authority of rank.

Peter Drucker

Objectives of the Routine Maintenance Process

The Routine Maintenance Process (RMP) is the maintenance business process by which all the day-to-day maintenance is accomplished. This process includes proactive (predictive and preventive) and reactive (repair) maintenance. The participants in this process typically include a maintenance foreman or supervisor, craftsmen, a representative from the group that operates the equipment, and several others. Depending on the size of the facility and the number of independent operations it has, there can be a significant number of people working together to share resources and coordinate work, using a common priority system and a common resource pool.

I have found that the RMP is the most difficult of all maintenance business processes to keep effective over time. There are probably a number of reasons. To accurately describe the objectives of the RMP it is important to understand the issues that make it difficult to implement and maintain. To be effective over the long haul, the RMP needs to include elements that address those issues.

The following are the most commonly cited reasons for difficulty or failure:

- RMP involves the greatest number of people.
- The participants have different priorities.
- The participants have competing priorities.
- RMP is an on-going or "evergreen" activity so it is difficult to organize and energize a single "push" that will carry through to completion.
- Emergency situations have a disruptive effect that makes recovery difficult.
- Frequently average performers are assigned to the RMP. Higher performers are assigned to more urgent or visible activities.

Some of these characteristics may be assigned to your own RMP and you may agree that they contribute to shortcomings, but I believe that several more subtle problems also exist.

1. The RMP depends on individuals making the proper choice when comparing current risk to longer-term value.

2. Individuals empowered to make those choices are poorly equipped to make wise choices.

3. Organizations tend to reward highly visible "fire-fighters". The individuals who put their efforts into prevention and who never allow "fires" to get started remain invisible, and go unrewarded.

Let's discuss each of these problems individually.

Considering the first point, most plants are more reactive than they need to be. It is necessary to be reactive when something bad has happened, or when something bad can be prevented by fast action. There is a difference between having an increased risk of failure, and being on a path to a failure.

Let's use a simple example to illustrate this point. Say your plant has both a primary and a spare feed pump. If the primary pump fails, the spare pump starts. If both pumps fail at the same time, the plant shuts down. Let's assume the plant is making $1 million per day so nobody wants the plant to shut down.

Now, let's assume that both pumps have a MTBF (mean time between failures) of ten years. In other words, the reliability is approximately 90% and the unreliability is approximately 10%. When both pumps are serviceable in the parallel redundant configuration, the combined reliability of the set is approximately 99% and the unreliability is 1%. This means that there is a 1% likelihood that feed pumps will cause an outage in any one year period. Or, there is a 0.0027% likelihood of failure in any single day. If the plant is making $1 million per day, the "dollarized" risk is $27.30 per day.

Now let's assume that the primary pump fails so that the spare pump is started. Let's further assume that the spare pump is performing well. There is no vibration, leakage from the seal, or other unusual conditions.

What action should you take with respect to the repair of the primary pump?

a. Declare the repair of the primary pump an emergency and work round the clock to repair it.
b. Work the repair ahead of all routine work, but not round the clock.
c. Work as routine and repair on a first-in, first-out basis.

Most effective RMPs are designed to handle instances like this, using alternative b. without sacrificing efficiency or effectiveness. Few people who are aggressive enough to be placed in a position of responsibility over a plant making $1 million a day would consider alternative c. So, in reality, we only need to compare alternative a. and alternative b.

Let's start by doing the math that describes the current risk for operating the plant with a single feed pump. The MTBF is still ten years because the spare pump is in good shape. The reliability of the feed pump service is 90% and the unreliability is 10%. There is thus a 0.027% likelihood of failure in any single day. The "dollarized" risk is $273.97 per day.

Let's assume that an "emergency" repair (working round-the-clock and repairing only the specific problem area) will require two days. Let's also assume that an "accelerated" repair (move to the front of the line, work on days only, and perform a comprehensive reconditioning) will require seven days. The total value of the risk in the first instance is approximately $548, and the total value of the risk in the second instance is $1918.00. The "saved" operational risk by working round-the-clock is therefore $1370.00.

Now consider the other side of the coin. What additional costs are introduced by working the pump on an emergency basis? There are three forms of added cost:

1. Cost of overtime and ineffectiveness due to working off shifts.
2. Cost of lost effectiveness due to interrupting current plans.
3. Cost of added risk due to reduced reliability resulting from a hurried repair.

Let's quantify each of these costs.

First, if the repair is completed in two days we can assume that four of the six shifts are overtime shifts. Over the two days there will be two "Day shifts," two "swing shifts" and two "graveyard shifts". It is reasonable to expect that the effectiveness of a day shift is 1.0. The effectiveness of the swing shift is 0.75 and the effectiveness of the graveyard shift is 0.50.

Let's assume that crews of two craftsmen are working on this job each shift that the straight-time hourly rate is $20.00 per hour, and the overtime rate is $30.00 per hour.

To determine the cost, benefit, and waste in this situation we need to understand that the amount of work being done on the pump is less than a complete re-conditioning. The effective hours spent on the pump are calculated by the formula:

Effective hours = Crew size X hours per shift X number of shifts X effectiveness

For the two day shifts this equals:
$$2 \times 8 \times 2 \times 1.0 = 32 \text{ mh}$$

For the two swing shifts this equals:
$$2 \times 8 \times 2 \times 0.75 = 24 \text{ mh}$$

For the two graveyard shifts this equals:
$$2 \times 8 \times 2 \times 0.5 = 16 \text{ mh}$$

The total number of "effective" man-hours equals:
$$32 + 24 + 16 = 72 \text{ mh}$$

Had this job been worked in the same manner as days, it would have cost:
$$72 \times \$20.00 = \$1440.00.$$

The "value" of this job the "way it was performed" is $1440.00. The value of a complete, high-quality refurbishment is more, but this job probably only changed a seal or a single bearing.

Now let's calculate what the job actually cost.

Day Shift
$$2 \times 8 \times 2 \times \$20.00 = \$640.00$$

Swing Shift
$$2 \times 8 \times 2 \times \$30.00 = \$960.00$$

Graveyard Shift
$$2 \times 8 \times 2 \times \$30.00 = \$960.00$$

The total actual cost is: 640 + 960 + 960 = $2560.00. (This calculation is without consideration for other costs like paid lunches during all shifts.)

So the "wasted" cost for working round the clock is: $2560 − $1440 = $1120

Second, let's calculate the value of lost effectiveness. We will make a simplifying assumption that the maintenance schedules will be able to recover effectiveness after the first day, so only one day of impact will be considered.

We will assume that the individuals assigned to work on the day shift are reassigned from planned and scheduled jobs so they will lose two hours effectiveness per person due to being reassigned. Experience tells us that is not an unrealistic loss. Also assume that the two individuals working graveyard shifts will not be available for the next day, so the work they were assigned to perform will have to be re-assigned. Again we will assume two hours loss per person.

The total cost of loss effectiveness is:

Day shift: 2 people for 2 hours X $20.00 = $80.00
Graveyard shift 2 people for 2 hours X $20.00 = $80.00
Total lost effectiveness $160.00

Finally, let's calculate the added cost due to unreliability. This calculation is fairly difficult. The ten year MTBF is likely built on performing something akin to precision maintenance, which requires restoring original tolerances, fits, and clearances. Companies that fall into the trap of repeatedly fixing only what is broken rather than restoring the inherent reliability, frequently have MTBF for pumps of two years or so. With this new MTBF, the reliability of the primary pump is 61% and the reliability of the set (primary and spare pump) is now 96%.

As a result, the risk of failure has been increased by 3% per year until the pump is brought back to inherent reliability. Let's assume that the pump is half-way through its typical 15-year life so there will be 5 years of added risk. The impact of a failure will be the cost of an emergency repair. (Let's use 2 days production) $2 million.

The following table is used to convert each year's risk to present value. The total risk is the sum of all present values (using an earning power of 10%)

Year	Increased Likelihood of Failure	Impact of Failure	Risk	Present Value of Future Risk
1	3%	$2M	$60K	$54.5K
2	3%	$2M	$60K	$49.5K
3	3%	$2M	$60K	$45.0K
4	3%	$2M	$60K	$41.0K
5	3%	$2M	$60K	$37.3K
			Total PV	$227.3K

The total present value of the decision to work the pump round the clock is:

Added Overtime	$ 1120.00
Labor effectiveness	$ 160.00
Lost reliability	$ 227,300.00
Total	$ 228,580.00

This cost is intended to save $1370.00 in current risk. Even when comparing current costs only (1120 + 160 = $1280.00), the decision is of marginal value. When viewing the decision to work round-the-clock from a long term perspective, the choice is a dead-loser.

The data in the table of annual cost of risk reminds us that when we have made short sighted choices, the best thing we can do is to reverse the decision as soon as possible. The sooner we can properly repair the pump to restore the inherent reliability, the better.

Getting back to the points made at the start of the chapter I said that there were three subtle problems that make the RMP hard to keep effective.

The preceding example tends to support both the first and second point.

Plant managements will often choose to work a breakdown round the clock because of the perceived current risks. When comparing the value of the current risk to the value of the larger term costs and impacts, the choice is inappropriate.

The second point was that people in positions of power do not understand the issues. Ask yourself, how many of the people in your current organization who make these decisions would perform the analysis described above? Now ask yourself how many of them would know how to perform the above analysis? Finally ask yourself how many would understand the above analysis if it were prepared for them?

For most plants, the answers would be none, a very few, and some, but not the majority. As a result, plants with "successful" RMP's typically set rules for handling emergency work, break-ins, or schedule interruptions. In one way or another, people causing the interruption are held accountable for their choices. They need to explain why they made their choices to someone who can make a difference, like the plant manager.

The third thing that makes an effective RMP difficult to implement and maintain is our reward system. We tend to reward people we see as very active and those who seem to "save our bacon". I have never observed it any other way than this. We might say we reward the people who stay ahead of the problems, but that is not how we act. Companies may give their proactive performers a percent or two larger raises each year, but they promote the highly visible fire-fighters. Unless and until they stop acting in a manner that rewards those who allow fires to get started, people will remain highly reactive.

Now that we have discussed the things that make the RMP difficult to install and remain effective, let's discuss what an RMP is and how it works.

Elements of the Routine Maintenance Process

Let's begin the description of the RMP by providing a process map for work that is accomplished in a "normal manner". In using the work "normal", I am including both emergency and high-priority work that flows through the process as it is designed.

> **Design for the "rule" not the "exception":**
> It is important to design a work management process to deal with the "rule" or typical work rather than for the "exception". If 95% or more of all work can be handled in a highly-efficient system, why build in features that add inefficiency to the 95% for the sake of the other 5%? Build a system that allows the majority of work to flow efficiently and adds complexity for only the small portion of work that justifies added complexity and inefficiency.

Process Map

The following Process Map describes the steps through which "normal" routine maintenance work will pass.

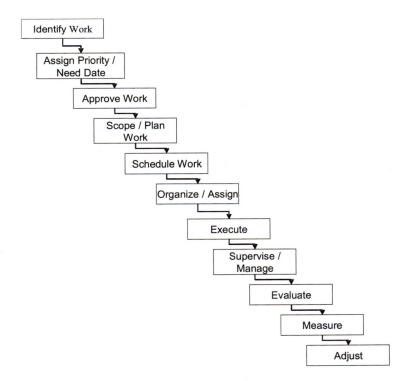

The work management process for routine maintenance work begins with identifying the work and concludes with identifying any adjustments needed to make the process more effective or efficient. There are "loops" that can be added to this process map. An example of a "loop" would be a step that returns disapproved work to the originator with an explanation of why it was rejected. This loop would have the benefits of making the originator understand why his recommendation was not accepted. This loop as well as others could be added. For the sake of simplicity, I have left it to the readers to identify the loops that are appropriate for their organizations.

Process Clock

In order to set a basis upon which other features of this process will be built, let's describe the "assumed" Process Clock at this time.

Let's assume our Process Clock has the following features:

- The only "scheduled" crew is on day shifts and week days only.
- The day shift will begin at 8:00 am each day and end at 4:30pm each day. There is an informal break for fifteen minutes at 10:00am, a formal 30 minute lunch break at noon and an informal fifteen-minute afternoon break at 2:00pm.
- First-start jobs will start promptly at 8:00am each day. Emergency work that has been identified overnight will interrupt first-start jobs only if they were important enough to call out work-force the night before.
- First-start jobs and all other jobs for each day will be identified in a 15-minute scheduling meeting that occurs at 2:00pm on the preceding day.
- Emergency work will continue round the clock until

completed.
- High-priority work can continue on evening and week-end shifts when it is most efficient to do so.

As procedures and protocols are developed and adminis-tered, they should keep the intent of the process clock in mind.

Process Descriptors

In the earlier chapter describing the elements of a work-management process the following descriptors were identified:
- Why
- What
- Who
- When
- Where

Let's continue the development of the RMP by exploring the issues that should be addressed by those descriptors. You're probably beginning to recognize that at each step, we are adding more details to the shape and description of our RMP. The value in going through this effort is that, by clearly defining the boundaries of the process, we can clarify both how it is intended to function and how it is intended not to function. This information will help us cre-ate a highly-effective and efficient work management process.

Why

This process is intended to describe the handling of "normal" maintenance activities. It is not intended to handle tasks that have unusual requirements. Tasks with unusual requirements should be assigned to a Project Manager who can deal with all unusual aspects while not constricting the routine maintenance system.

What

This system is intended to handle maintenance. Tasks that do other than "put something back the way it was" should be handled elsewhere. When done properly, the RMP provides a good filter for "changes". Changes typically require some form of engineering resource that is not part of the RMP.

How

It is expected that individuals who are participants in this process will use the process "as currently designed". If something does not work well, they will formally change the process, not simply wander off and act independently.

Who

The participants in this process are the individuals named in the Accountability-Responsibility Matrix. Apart from those listed in the ARM, Plant Management is expected to support the process, its protocols and the discipline needed to make it effective. This process is designed to interface with the current organizational structure. If the organizational structure is changed, the RMP will need to be modified to account for the changes.

When

This process is designed to interface with the assumed Process Clock. If any aspect of the Process Clock is changed, the RMP will need to be modified to account for the differences.

Where

This process is designed to provide consistent proce-dures for all groups that currently share the same resource base to ensure that all participants justify and manage resources based on the same priorities.

Detailed Process Steps

Although it is beyond the scope of this book to describe each and every process step in detail, I will pick a few steps to indicate the kind of detail needed.

"Work Identification – Malfunction Report"

In most situations, the person initiating a work order is able only to identify a function (that is no longer fulfilling requirements) and a behavior (that is different from expected). For instance, when you take your car to the shop, you tell them that the engine is hesitating when it is cold. You do not tell them to adjust the timing or adjust the automatic choke. In some instances the initiator can describe the desired task or the desired end product. In those instances, the initiator should be warned to be cer-tain he knows what he wants because he will get what he has requested. If he simply wants something fixed he should only attempt to describe the affected function and the current behavior.

Much like visiting your family doctor, using a clear and complete description of symptoms leads to a more accurate diagnosis sooner. In preparing the Malfunction Report, the initiator should be asked to provide a clear and complete description of the failure. It is best to characterize most of the possible Malfunction Reports using a set of look up tables. Keep in mind that it is best for each and every field on the work order to be "sortable". If the malfunction notification or work description field is completely "free-form", it will be difficult to easily process the data for valuable information in the future. Even if all the information cannot be reduced to look-up-tables or standard format, there are elements that can be. They include:

- Equipment Number
- Date/Time
- Impact of failure (e.g. outage, reduced output, switch to spare, etc)
- Others including plan, location, account number.

In summary, the Work Identification-Malfunction Report steps should include the following descriptions:

- Identify affected equipment by number
- Identify Date and Time of Failure
- Identify impact of failure if known
- Describe affected function
- Describe unusual behavior
- Describe any other unusual conditions at the time of failure or immediately prior.

"Prioritization and Scheduling"

Two elements of the RMP that fit closely together are the system for assigning priorities and the system for scheduling. It seems that most systems for assigning priorities have been developed by engineers who are anal compulsive. They end up with an alphabet soup of priorities that describe every subtle nuance that can affect the time when the work should be done. Provision of this data is confusing and unnecessary.

If you were to ask the people who schedule and perform the work what they would like, they would want to know two things:

1. Which tasks are emergencies that need to be done now?
2. If not an emergency, when does it need to be done?

If the maintenance organization were able to keep up with all the demands for routine maintenance instantly, it would result in the most responsive system. On the other hand, instantly responding to all requests does not acknowledge the fact that resource availability is typically a constant. Instant response would require a flexible resource supply that could expand and contract as needed. That amount of response would be uneconomic and impractical.

A priority system that blends the responsiveness of the priority system described above with recognition that resource availability is not "elastic" is described by the following:

1. **Emergency work** is started as soon as the job can be safely staged and materials can be assembled. This response typically does <u>not</u> result in taking people off currently assigned jobs.
2. **High priority work** takes precedence over routine work but is planned and scheduled to be accomplished within the next work week.
3. **Routine work** is accomplished in the order in which it is identified. When a new task is approved it is simply added to the end of the current schedule.

Some CMMS's contain scheduling tools that are compatible or easily adaptable to the scheduling that will result from this priority system. The scheduling system contains three tiers:

1. **Routine work**-Schedule by adding tasks at the end of the current backlog. Fill the schedule to 80% of the resource availability.
2. **High Priority work**- Schedule by adding tasks into slots within the next week. Fill the schedule to 95% of resource availability.
3. **Emergency work**-Schedule by adding tasks in the next day or the current wok period. The schedule should allow for 5% Emergency Work and when added, all available resources will be used.

Two points are not explicit from the above description. The first point involves instances where more than 5% of the resource is needed for emergency work. In this system, it is assumed that the additional resource will be supplied by overtime. If the work is truly emergency work, it will be necessary to work round-the-clock until the work is complete anyway.

The second point involves instances where there is not enough either emergency or high-priority work to consume 20% of the resource availability. In that situation, routine work will be pulled forward and scheduled sooner than expected. In a well-organized maintenance process, this situation occurs more often than one might expect. It never results in complaints. The only concern is with equipment preparation and job staging. If the schedule is being pulled forward, preparations need also to be addressed earlier.

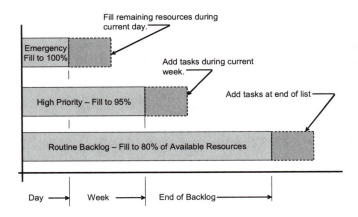

"Scoping and Planning Work"

After all is said and done, the only reason for organizing your RMP is to provide an opportunity for planning and scheduling. Studies have shown that unplanned and poorly scheduled work can consume as much as four times the amount of resources as well-planned and well-scheduled work. As a result, one key objective should be to have all work planned and all work tightly scheduled.

It is worthwhile asking, "What constitutes adequate planning?" When I have asked that question of individuals involved at different levels of the RMP, the response is most often a blank stare. The reason for the response is that they know what they currently do, but they have never considered what is required.

The simplest definition of what constitutes adequate planning is the following. All individuals performing an adequately-planned job can go to the job site and perform all tasks related with the job without interruption. That means they have all the proper tools, and materials. They have all the procedures and instructions. All permits and preparations have been properly completed. In other words, the job should "come off like clockwork".

If all jobs have been properly planned it will be possible to assemble tight and accurate schedules. The crew size and number of hours required will be included in each job plan. Using that information it will be possible to build a schedule that uses all available resources while accomplishing jobs in accordance with requested priorities and completion dates.

Again, asking the question, "What constitutes a tight schedule?" can aid in determining the end product we want to achieve. A tight schedule is one that uses all available resources without gaps or unproductive periods. This result can only happen when you know how much time each job should require and you fill all the work hours available from your workforce.

Returning to the discussion of Scoping and Planning work, this element of the RMP is something of an enigma. When asked if they perform planning, most every plant or shop will say they do. However, if you suggest a program to improve planning skills, they will resist saying, "they do it all the time".

In fact, people in many plants and shops, while knowing how to plan, do it with such irregularity and with so little discipline that it has little impact on effectiveness and efficiency.

As an example think about a situation where only 20% of all jobs are unplanned. In this situation, one in five jobs will need to interrupt planned and scheduled jobs to obtain resources. Say four planned jobs need to use a hydraulic crane for two hours each and the crane is scheduled sequentially from one job to the next. Now say that an unplanned job is allowed to interrupt the planned work. It is likely that all four jobs will be delayed and possible that all four jobs will be cancelled. It takes very little poorly-planned and scheduled work to contaminate an entire maintenance program.

So what standard should be applied? Generally speaking, effective planning is a two- step process consisting of scoping (conducted at the work site) and planning (assembled in an office).

Job scoping is an activity in which the entire job scope is defined. There is only one way to do this and it entails a trip to the work site. The appendix includes an example of a work scoping form that can be adapted to the specific needs of your plant or shop.

One approach is for the work planner to have a tablet of work scoping forms on a clipboard. Each morning he should print out all the work orders that need to be planned that day. He can then take a few minutes to organize them into a route that will allow him to visit all work sites sequentially in a relatively short amount of time. While visiting each site the planner should make note of any specific requirements that will need to be addressed. For instance:

- Will scaffolding be required
- Will lifting equipment be needed
- Will special tools (not typically carried by mechanics) be needed?
- Will special personal protective equipment be needed?
- Etc.

The back of the scoping sheet provides room for preparing a sketch of the job site. After visiting the site, the planner should be able to return to his office and assemble a complete and accurate plan from his work station.

The comprehensive work plan may include any or all of the following items:
1. Work order
2. Sequential Task Description
3. Blinding/isolation Plan

4. Scaffolding Plan/Sketch
5. Tool list
6. Material list
7. Parts list
8. Lifting and Rigging requirements
9. Rental Equipment
10. Etc.

As arrangements are made or commitments are received, records may be added to the work order file.

Clearly, there are jobs that will require only a small file and limited planning. For instance, a task to replace a small gasket in a water system that can be easily isolated should require limited planning. In this example, the craft may carry all the needed tools. It is possible that gaskets are readily available from a "gasket board" in the area shop. On the other hand, I have seen jobs like the one described above require several re-works or result in multiple delays and extended use of resources because the wrong gasket was replaced, an improper gasket was installed, or the need for a scaffold was not anticipated.

Had those jobs been "scoped" and a plan prepared based on details in the scoping form, no waste or delay would have occurred.

"Evaluate, Measure and Adjust"

After a difficult day, most people are just glad it is over. Rather than trying to figure out why it was so difficult, they are satisfied to put it behind them and start fresh tomorrow. That approach is probably acceptable when the reason for the difficulties has been something unusual and is unlikely to happen again. But when you are getting a feeling of déjà vu, you need to call for a "time-out" and determine the cause of the problem.

Many work processes include simple evaluation forms that provide a mechanism to highlight any delays or situations producing waste. The following is an example of a form that RMP participants may use to report situations they feel should be corrected:

The objective is not to create a paperwork monster that requires an army to process. The objective is to create an expectation that people should complain when they see waste or delays. It also provides an outlet for frustration that otherwise continues to simmer.

```
                                                    Date:

    ☐ Delay
         * How Long _____
         * Crew Size _____
         * Why


    ☐ Waste
         * What was wasted _____
         * Approximate Value _____
         * Why



         Signed:_____
```

All effective business processes have several key measures that tell when the process is healthy. The health of the RMP can be determined by several key measures including:

- Percentage of Emergency work
- Percentage of Work Planned
- Schedule Attainment
- Schedule Compliance
- Crew Size divided by Work Input Rate

The meaning of those KPI's will be discussed later. For now it will suffice to say it is mandatory that:

1. KPI's be produced every week.
2. KPI's are accurate
3. Attention is given to them
4. Action is taken to drive them in the right direction

While KPI's may be produced and discussed only once each week, providing that the information needed to produce them is an on-going requirement. Work hours, materials, and parts, need to be properly assigned to every job. Each job needs to be assigned to the proper equipment. All jobs need to be properly closed each day to ensure that all information and all reports are timely and accurate.

The final step associated with the RMP is the "adjustment" step. Efficiency requires adjustment. No two consecutive weeks, and few consecutive days, require the same amount of resources. If the amount of resources working within a plant or shop remains the same day in and day out, there are either too many or too few. Bad things would typically begin happening if there were too few, so it is more likely there are too many. Too many resources means that things are not being managed as efficiently as they should be.

Accountability-Responsibility Matrix

Think for a moment about all the descriptions provided thus far in this chapter. For the most part, they describe work and how it fits into your system and organization. Although that information is helpful, think about how a maintenance supervisor views his job. A person in that position is interested in how to perform his job and what he needs to do to be successful. Stated in a more direct manner, each person wants to know the tasks for which he is accountable and for which he is responsible. A person's overall performance may be evaluated, based on other factors (attitude, creativity, etc.), but the primary basis should be quality of execution of accountabilities and responsibilities.

Each element of the RMP has a number of associated tasks. Each task needs to have one person identified as being accountable and one or more persons identified as being responsible. A typical Accountability-Responsibility Matrix (ARM) lists all the members of the team that are associated with the RMP. The benefit of listing all participants is that the list tells who is not involved in an activity as well as those who are involved. The chart below is an example involving the Scoping and Planning element of the RMP. This example of an ARM assumes that the following individuals are involved in the RMP.

- Maintenance Foreman
- Maintenance Planner

- Maintenance Craft
- Maintenance Scheduler
- Material Foreman
- Operations-Maintenance Coordinator
- Operator

As discussed earlier, the individual shown as being "accountable" is the primary focal
point for the task. In addition to
the individual shown as being
accountable, one or more
other individuals share "responsibility" for making each
task a success. In a team, it is
unacceptable to allow your
team-mate to fail.

An ARM needs to be constructed for each element of the
RMP, and each element of the RMP must be broken
down into the tasks needed to achieve its objectives. The
specific positions in our organization must be included.
The ones shown in the example may be similar to those
in your organization, but it is not intended to portray an
optimum organization.

Roles for Each Individual

As mentioned in the last section, much of the work-management process description is dedicated to describing
the flow of work through the process. In fact, most of the
tools used in developing and describing a work management process focus on how work is handled.

Accountability - Responsibility - Matrix

Scoping and Planning

	Maintenance Foreman	Maintenance Planner	Maintenance Scheduler	Maintenance Craft	Operations-Maintenance Coordinator	Operator	Material Planner	Crane Foreman
1. Print list of unplaned work for each planner.	R	R	A					
2. Organize list of unplanned work by location - create a path.	R	A						
3. Visit work sites and prepare scoping form for each job.	R	A					R	R
4. Plan each job.	R	A		R				
5. Prepare Work Pack	R	R	A				R	
6. Estimate crew size and man-hours for each task.	A	R	R	R				
7. Prepare lifting plan and size lifting equipment.	R							A
8. Order materials and identify delivery date.	R	R					A	

In the last section, the ARM began to move the focus from the work to the people involved in executing the work. Continuing that transition from work to people, we will look at "Role Descriptions". Each and every individual involved in the RMP needs to have a role description. The role description needs to clearly define the results expected of each position in the RMP organization.

Once the ARM has been completed it is possible to simply extract the accountabilities and responsibilities for each position. For example, the Maintenance Foreman may have a role similar to the chart on the next page.

Once each individual understands the concept of "accountability" and the concept of "responsibility" and has a complete list of tasks from the ARM's for each element of the RMP, their roles should be clear.

In addition to the information in a spreadsheet like the one on the next page, it is often necessary to provide supplementary details. For instance, it there are special ways in which a task should be done, it is best to avoid confusion by providing added detail in written procedures.

Instruction for Using IT Systems

I recall a situation in which the company spent a great deal of time and money updating and implementing the RMP using a well-known CMMS. The system was working well and everyone seemed happy with the results. Within two years, the company decided to change to an enterprise-wide information system in part to address

Role Description		
Maintenance Foreman		
	Accountability	Responsibility
Identify Work		
- Check CMMS for duplicate work.	A	
- Verify proper equipment identity.	A	
Assign Priority / Need Date		
Approve Work		
- Verify approval before processing		R
Scope / Plan Work		
- Initiate planning new WOs within 3 days		R
- Perform scoping and tasking		R
- Create material list		R
- Estimate crew size and man-hours	A	
- Order materials in a timely manner		R
- Plan mobile and lifting equipment		R
- Verify accounting codes		R
- Build work packages		R
Schedule Work		
- Identify "ready-to-schedule" work		R
- Identify " ready-to-execute" work		R
- Prepare weekly schedule		R
- Prepare daily schedule	A	
- Identify "first-start" jobs	A	
- Identify who will be assigned each job	A	
- Communicate problems preventing "first start" jobs	A	
Organize / Assign Work		
- Pre-stage tools	A	
- Pre-stage materials	A	
- Line up crafts on complex jobs in advance	A	
- Coordinate multi-craft jobs between crafts	A	
- Coordinate jobs requiring mobile/liftine equipment	A	
- See all permirts are available on time		R
Supervise / Manage Work		
- Assign full day of work to each craft every day	A	
- Assign first start jobs	A	
- Identify and eliminate job barriers	A	
- See permits are issued on time		R
- See permits are signed upon completion		R
Measure Results		
- Complete a "Delay Report" on all job delays		R
- Record accurate start time and finish time for all jobs	A	
- Enter accurate charged man-hours into CMMS	A	
- Sign off Work Order when complete	A	
Adjust		
- Review all Job Delay forms for your area	A	
- Identify chronic problems	A	
- Develop and implement corrective action plans		R

Y2K concerns. This enterprise-wide system included a new CMMS. The features of the new CMMS program were unlike the old system. The new system offered the benefit of enhanced integration, but its application and use was not intuitive.

A few months after the new IT System was installed I visited the plant and asked the staff to describe how the new system was working. At the conclusion of their description, it was clear that all scheduling was being done on a white-board and they were no longer performing any planning.

This story provides what might seem to be an extreme example of the importance of integrating the IT system with the WMP it supports. The example might seem extreme, but the opposite is true. Think about a situation where McDonald's restaurants begin selling BLT's (Bacon-Lettuce-Tomato sandwiches) without modifying their systems. There would be no automated pricing from the register. There would be no automated ordering between the register and the food preparation area. There would be no automated replenishment of inventory. The lack of IT system integration would cause inefficiencies. Now think about how many IT systems are as closely integrated as the Mc Donald's example, very few.

Rather than being an extreme example of an unlikely scenario, poor IT system integration is the norm. Taking the time to see that the IT systems are closely integrated with the process is well worth the effort.

Characteristics of the RMP

In addition to the procedures and charts needed to completely describe the elements of the RMP, there are some further characteristics that should be integrated into your organization and culture.

Adapt Individual Schedules to Process Requirements

As mentioned earlier, the work-management process is a description of how work flows and is accomplished. Also, I mentioned earlier that, it is important to provide role descriptions describing the tasks and objectives that each individual is expected to achieve. For a moment think about how a specific individual will fit all those tasks into his daily work schedule. For example, what does he do at 7:00am? What does he do at 7:30am, and 8:00am and 9:00am and the rest of the day? In order to complete all the tasks each individual needs to arrange his day in a specific order.

Now think about two people who have to meet at specific times during the day but have vastly different tasks to complete, and different schedules. Now think of an entire team of people who have to meet at a specific time during the day. All members of this group have different roles and only one thing in common. They all need to be ready to meet to discuss the following day's schedule at the chosen time.

My point is that for the process to work, each individual needs to adapt his schedule to support the needs of the process. For instance, if the Maintenance Foreman meets with the Operations-Maintenance Coordinator at 7:00am and 11:00am and both of them meet with all other individuals in similar roles at their plant at 2:00pm; they will need to learn how to schedule all their other tasks around those meetings. That doesn't happen by itself.

Have you ever noticed when one of your "first string player" is on vacation and a back-up is taking his place, things get a little ragged. That is because the back-up hasn't learned how to manage all the tasks around the required schedule.

Making individual's schedules fit together seems to go best when it is facilitated by an outside party who has no favorites and just wants to get things organized.

Integrated with Customers' Needs

Why are some companies more successful than other companies who sell the same product? Why is it you would prefer to pay more to some companies for the exact same product?

The answer is that some companies put their customers first. They don't say, "This is what we have, take it or leave it." Instead they say, "How can we help you?"

There is a big difference in attitude when you view your customer as being important to your success than when you take the position that, "We are the only game in town."

In the RMP, the operating department is the customer of the maintenance department. In most plants the maintenance department "assumes" they know what their customer wants, so they never ask.

Benefits of asking your customer what they want Include:

- It gives you an opportunity to provide what they really want.
- It provides an opportunity to tell your customer what out-of-the-ordinary services actually cost.
- It may create an opportunity to fulfill requirements at less cost by more clearly defining what is required.

Integration with Support Organizations

As with integration of the RMP with customer needs, there is also a need, and indeed opportunities, associated with better integration of the RMP with the organizations that support it.

Philosophically, one might say that the business process or work management process of any organization can be no more effective than the processes of the organizations that it supports. For instance, if I am an organization that is a supplier to a maintenance department that is very reactive, by nature I will need to be reactive. If they wake up in a new world everyday, in many ways, I am destined to wake with them in that same world.

The opposite is also true. As the maintenance organization introduces concepts of maintenance excellence and becomes more proactive and better planned and organized, all the organizations that support that department can also become more effective.

Let's discuss two examples:

1. If I have a scheduling horizon that is nominally one week out in the future for all routine work, there is no need for the purchasing organization to ware house the supplies to support that work on-site. That material can be left in supplier warehouses till needed and then delivered as part of routine deliveries.
2. If I have introduced a significant number of predictive and preventive tasks, then it is possible to time the delivery of parts for those tasks for shortly before they are scheduled to be needed.

Once the maintenance processes become better planned and less reactive, all the plant or shop departments that interact with maintenance can optimize their business processes.

Leaning Out the End-Product

Anyone who has been involved with "Lean" or "Lean-Six-Sigma" initiatives recognizes one significant problem at the very start. The problem is that many activities and transactions are conducted without the benefit of an organized and documented business process. There is a general concept of how things get done, but when you try to identify ways to decrease waste and increase consistency the response will be, "Oh, we do that!" or "We tried that for a while but I don't know why we stopped." In other words, there is no real process in existence.

In fact, many organizations intuitively know how to do things in a more organized or more efficient manner, but they don't do it because one or a few of the participants don't want to do it that way. Or because it is impossible to get everyone to agree on how to do something when everything depends on spoken words and the spoken words change with each person and every time they are repeated.

A well-organized and well-document work-management process provides a strong foundation upon which significant improvements can be based. When things are done in a structured, consistent, and disciplined manner, waste becomes more apparent. When dumb things are done in a repetitive way, people begin to ask, "Why?'

Discipline

Another important characteristic of an effective RMP is "discipline." An analogy best describes this. If you were to assemble a group of the most physically-talented football players in the world, they would not be successful until they coordinated their efforts around a specific set of plays.

When they become organized, they would start winning games. Now let's say that one of the players decided he knew better than the system and started to do things his own way. If he were on defense, he would allow openings to exist. If he were on offense, he would miss blocks or be in the wrong place to make blocks.

The RMP is much the same. It depends on a group of people working together as a team. If individuals do not fulfill their accountabilities or do not support team mates in areas of assigned responsibilities, the team will not be effective.

There are then only two alternatives:
1. The person needs to correct the behavior.
2. The person needs to be replaced.

Evergreen

Every business process or work management process becomes dated and needs to evolve. If for no other reason than to refresh the feeling of ownership by the current participants it is necessary to keep the RMP "evergreen."

Although it is a costly, time-consuming, and unsettling effort to totally re-engineer the RMP, it is important to always to be open to the need for changes.

There needs to be some mechanism included in RMP administration that facilitates and even invites suggested improvements and modernization.

Mechanism for Feeding Entropy

As was discussed in an earlier chapter, it seems there is always some amount of energy that is aimed at "undoing" the RMP or any other work management process.

To counter that natural energy, you need to consciously invest the same or a greater amount of energy to keep things together. The last section discussed keeping the RMP "evergreen". The energy invested in performing routine audits, monitoring Key Performance Indicators, studying and implementing process improvements, and performing Lean or Lean Six-Sigma initiatives, form a majority of the effort needed to keep the RMP effective and efficient. These efforts can also highlight any deterioration resulting from the natural effect of "entropy."

Additional Thoughts from References

Nyman, Don and Levitt, Joel; Maintenance Planning, Scheduling and Coordination; Industrial Press, New York; 2001

> As mentioned in the Introduction, the objective of the Little Black Book of Maintenance Excellence is to provide a comprehensive yet high level description of all the significant elements of Maintenance Excellence. As such, the reader is directed to more detailed texts on specific subjects if he is interested in learning more. This referenced text provides excellence details concerning planning and scheduling as a part of the Routine Maintenance Process.

> The whole objective of going to the time and expense of implementing the Routine Maintenance Process is to provide the opportunity for all work to be planned and once the work is thoroughly planned to assemble a tight and efficient schedule. Although this book has

provided the reader with some thoughts on how best to plan work and how to assemble a schedule, a great deal more can be said on the subject. The referenced text provides some excellent thoughts for the reader to consider.

Wireman, Terry; Computerized Maintenance Management Systems; Industrial Press, New York; 1994

The Computerized Maintenance Management System (CMMS) is the heart of the Routine Maintenance process (RMP). If a process is cumbersome for individuals to use, they will use it poorly. Work will be poorly planned and poorly scheduled. In addition, critical resources will be consumed by coping with the CMMS rather than managing the work. Finally, critical information will be lost and over time, it will be impossible to analyze the cost of maintenance and the cost of poor reliability. Lacking that information, it will be impossible to justify needed improvements. The referenced text is a good one in helping the reader think through the characteristics needed in a CMMS and the ways in which the selected CMMS should be applied.

Wireman, Terry; World Class Maintenance Management; Industrial Press, New York; 1990

The referenced text provides the reader with additional insights into planning, scheduling and organizing the overall RMP.

Womack, James P. and Jones, Daniel T., Lean Thinking, Simon & Schuster, New York, 1996

One of the principle benefits of having a structured and disciplined RMP is the ability to identify waste and eliminate it. This text is useful in helping the reader think through the steps needed to "lean-out" the RMP and eliminate inefficiencies.

CHAPTER 5
THE TURNAROUND PROCESS

It doesn't work to leap a twenty-foot chasm
in two ten-foot jumps.
American proverb

The process used to prepare and conduct the regular renewal maintenance that is designed to ensure on-going reliable performance can have any of a number of names. Sometimes it is called an overhaul, sometimes a shutdown, sometimes an outage, and sometimes a turn-around.

For purposes of this discussion, I will use the following definitions:

1. A Turnaround is a planned activity involving an entire plant or facility that is intended to reset the clock on all affected equipment so the unit can complete the maximum possible production run without interruption.
2. An Outage is a planned activity involving only a portion of a plant or facility.
3. A Shutdown is an unplanned interruption with the typical response being to repair only the equipment that caused the interruption and restart as quickly as possible.

4. An Overhaul is a planned activity that involves only one specific item of equipment and is completed in a manner that resets the clock for that item so that it can complete the maximum possible run without interruption.

This discussion will focus on the Turnaround Process (TAP) specifically. The Outage Process and the Overhaul Process are special instances of the Turnaround Process that affect only a part of a plant or only a specific item of equipment.

As the proverb at the introduction is intended to suggest, conducting a successful turnaround is like leaping a broad chasm. It is impossible to do so in two jumps. Similarly, it is impossible to enter into a turnaround in a half-planned manner and complete it successfully. For that reason, many companies have decided to establish requirements to begin preparations for major turnarounds, eighteen months to two years in advance. In recent years, normal turnarounds have cost tens of millions of dollars. Those turnarounds that include major

One measure of adequacy for Turnaround planning is "optimization".

If you have started your turnaround preparations far enough in advance, you should have the opportunity to optimize the schedule, identify instances where more creative and aggressive plans can be developed and where the schedule can be modified to reduce the critical path duration.

modification projects can cost hundreds of millions of dollars. In these situations, all the planning and scheduling must be completed in advance.

As with the other work management processes described in this book, I will provide a high level description of the Turnaround Process. I will also provide a variety of other details that I believe are important to a successful process. However, this book is not intended to do justice to all the details needed to fully describe a comprehensive Turnaround Process. That subject would require a complete book by itself and are is recommended at the end of this chapter.

Elements of the Turnaround Process

The following list describes the steps for preparing and executing a turnaround (TA). Because of the length of time required for many of the activities, they will necessarily overlap and be done concurrently. On the other hand, the list has been prepared in the nominal order of their accomplishment. For instance, the person performing work must be appointed before the work can begin and all work must be identified and planned before a schedule can be assembled.

Turnaround Process Steps
1. Identify Turnaround Manager
2. Assemble Turnaround Team
3. Adapt TA Calendar and Control Document
4. Develop TA Premises
5. Assemble TA Worklist
6. Close TA Worklist

7. Initiate Cost Tracking/Forecasting System
8. Conduct Work-list Review
9. Order Long-Lead Materials
10. Conduct Detailed Planning
11. Develop/Release Bid Packages
12. Integrate Capital Projects
13. Develop SD and SU Plans
14. Develop Final Cost Estimate
15. Create Comprehensive Schedule
16. Assemble Work Packages
17. Conduct Management Review
18. Optimize Schedule and Job Plans
19. Release Purchase Orders and Rentals
20. Assemble Execution Team
21. Complete Field Staging
22. Initiate Work Add System
23. Begin Tracking Schedule/Costs
24. Begin Tracking Key Measures
25. Complete Turnaround
26. Critique Turnaround

The process steps provided above briefly describe the individual activities and the general sequence of events in preparing and executing a large turnaround.

Much like the RMP, the TAP has "loops" that involve decision points and steps that return to earlier activities for reprocessing. An example is when the TA is too costly or takes too long. It might then be necessary to reset the turnaround premises, reduce the scope, and develop a whole new schedule and budget. For the sake of simplicity, I have chosen not to describe all the possible "loops".

It should be apparent how far back in the process each loop will need to extend. Part of the reason for starting the turnaround preparations early is to allow time for relatively extensive rework without arriving at starting time for the turnaround with preparations still not complete.

Process Calendar

Unlike the RMP, the Turnaround Process requires both a Process Clock and a Process Calendar to adequately describe the issues of timing that must be addressed. The Process Clock will be addressed in the next section and deals with the actual times on a twenty-four hour, seven-day per week clock when repetitive events occur. The Process Calendar is the subject of this section and is dedicated to the timing of events stretching months or years prior to the Turnaround being prepared.

I recall a story I was told by the Maintenance Manager of a fairly large chemical plant. By way of background, this facility built a completely new unit several years previously and the story involved the first major turnaround. The unit was new and the technology involved in the process was new to most of the people at the facility, so the turnaround was a learning event for them.

The facility planners used a normal turnaround planning process, which included little lead time, and they considered few of the possibilities that might materialize. As might have been expected, the turnaround ended well over budget and weeks beyond the expected schedule. The plant personnel did their best to minimize the impact but the results were still bad.

After approximately 12 weeks of sixteen-hour days and seven-day weeks, the turnaround was finally over. Rather than giving the group some time to recover, the Operations VP and the Finance VP asked for a meeting to be held on the first Saturday following re-start. The Operations VP started the meeting by saying, "This turn-around has gone so far over budget, we are here to determine if you are totally incom-petent or if some of you have been embezzling funds."

The Maintenance Manager who told me the story said, "You never saw a group working so hard to prove they were incompetent."

Unfortunately, I was able to verify that this story was true from some of the other participants in the Saturday meeting.

I include this story under the heading of the Process Calendar because instances of turnaround performance like the one described above are not uncommon. And, they are most often the result of inadequate preparation.

To avoid these kinds of events, the question that needs to be answered is, "How much lead time is needed to adequately prepare for a turnaround?" In attempting to answer that question, there are several ways one can look at the challenge of preparing a comprehensive plan.

1. One way to look at lead time is to ask what work is being done and what major elements are being maintained or replaced. If those elements require lead time for engineering design, fabrication, job planning, lift planning, and integration with work in the surrounding area, the timing of advanced plans needs to include all these elements.

2. If this were a large project, how much time would be spent in preparation? Keep in mind that field planning and staging for most projects are done on a day-to-day basis. Because many projects work on much longer schedules than turn arounds, and because they typically work only single shifts, it is possible to dive into such a project with only a small fraction of detailed planning complete. That is not so with turnarounds. All planning needs to be completed before the turn around begins. If you were to think of the cumulative amount of planning (including planning completed after the start of the project), that would be needed for a project of comparable size, then move all that work prior to the turn around. How far in advance should preparations begin?

3. Another consideration for turnaround preparations is the amount of work required in terms of FTEs (full-time-equivalent) as compared to the portion of time individuals are allowed to devote to preparations. It is common for the TA Manager to be assigned full-time, but many of the other participants are assigned only part-time. They need

to conduct turnaround preparations at the same time as they are filling some other role. If a job takes a man-year to complete and only half the time of a person is available, it will be completed in two years.

4. Two other things to consider are; a. How complex is this turnaround compared with past turn arounds and b. How much of the preparations that were completed in the past and can be copied?

One thing about lead time, if you finish early, it is OK. If you finish late it is not.

Including all the pluses and minuses, many plants settle on a starting time of eighteen months prior to the anticipated starting date. They acknowledge this starting time by assigning the TA Manager. Some people may view this period as long, but it allows the TA Manager to begin analyzing the scope of the TA and adjusting the TA preparation TA calendar accordingly.

Rather than simply using a calendar, it is best to describe the timing of required events in a "control document". A control document is a spreadsheet that breaks down all the individual tasks associated with each element of the Process Map. For each of those tasks, a specific "accountable" individual is assigned as well as a "need date". In addition, a brief definition of the task is provided and a current status description. When completed, a completion date is shown so it will be clear when delays are happening and who is causing them. I have included an example of a Control Document.

Control Document

CD Manager						Date Last Updated:	7-Jan
Jack Ruby							

Item Number	Description	Assigned To:	Initial Date:	Due Date:	Current Status	System or EQ ID:	Status Code:
1	Assemble TA Premises	JFK	2-Jan	15-Jan	Complete	All	POS
2	Request TA Work Lists	JFK	2-Jan	15-Jan	Complete	All	POS
3	Conduct Work List Review	LCF	2-Jan	30-Jan	Currently scheduled for 1/22	All	POS
4	Publish Final Work List	JFK	2-Jan	15-Feb	Wait on Item 3	All	POS
5	Develop Shutdown Plan for Final Work List	LCF	15-Jan	1-Mar	Wait on Item 4	All	POS
6	Develop Flush Plan for Affected areas.	LCF	15-Jan	1-Mar	Wait on Item 4	All	POS
Etc.							

Status Code:	Definition	Color
POS	Progressing on schedule	Green
PBS	Progressing behind schedule	Yellow
L	Late	Red
C	Complete	Blue

Clearly, few TA Managers have administrative authority over all the individuals who contribute to a turnaround. As a result, the TA Manager must depend on others and hold them accountable. It is best to begin turnaround preparations by making a rule for control document activities. The rule is that it is OK to say you do not have time to complete your assignments. If you say that, the TA Manager will find another way to complete the work. If you do not take exception to the assignment, you are expected to complete the assignment on time. If you do not take exception, and do not complete the assignment on time, you are in trouble.

Some of the tasks on the control document are simply the element from the Process Map (like Assign TA Manager). Other elements from the Process Map may represent a number of tasks that will be assigned to several different people and should be shown as separate items on the control document.

For instance, Develop Shutdown (SD) and Start-Up (SU) Plan will have several parts:

1. Remove feed, empty, and decontaminate the unit.
2. Flush and remove hydrocarbons from the unit.
3. Install blinds and isolate.
4. Apply Lock Out/Tag Out devices and administrative controls.
5. Re-commission instruments
6. Remove blinds
7. Re-inventory the unit
8. Warm the unit
9. Start the unit – re-circulate off-spec material

10. Unit On-spec – begin shipping products

Plans for this range of activities are frequently developed by a team of personnel from Operations, Maintenance, Safety, and Engineering. In many plants, management tends to view units as being the responsibility of the Operations department while these tasks are occurring, so Operations personnel are assigned accountability for the development of these plans.

It is possible to calculate the completion date and start date for these tasks (and any other task) by counting back from the start date of the turnaround.

For instance:

1. Begin with the date the turnaround is expected to resume work.
2. Subtract the time needed for field staging – (people will be in the field working during this period, not planning, allow ~ one month)
3. Subtract the time needed to optimize the schedule and re-plan critical-path jobs, (allow ~ one month.)
4. Subtract time needed to combine all tasks in a single schedule and run the schedule (allow ~ one month to integrate all tasks and create a "smoothed" schedule).
5. Subtract the amount of time needed to develop these individual pieces. Unfortunately, there are aspects of each that tend to make them sequential. For example, it is necessary to complete the unit isolation plan before the Lock-Out-Tag-Out procedure. A reasonable estimate

for these four products is between two months and four months depending on the size of the units and the amount of well-documented experience.

Summing up the lead time described above, the step of developing shutdown and start up plans should begin at least six or seven months prior to the planned date for starting the turnaround. There are examples of situations where more resources can be assigned and the work can be completed in less time. There are also examples where a smaller portion of individuals' time is unavailable and activities should be started earlier.

It is best for the TA Manager to develop an understanding of the amount of resources that will be made available to the TA preparations. From that understanding, the TA Manager should calculate the projected lead-time for each step of the TA process. Once those dates are known, the TA Manager should create a control document that enables the tasks to be started in a timely manner and tracked through completion.

Process Clock

Any turnaround or outage represents a period of time when a significant "money-making" asset is out of service. Because of the economics, these events are worked on multiple shifts each day and, frequently on weekends as well as weekdays.

Most organizations are built to manage work eight hours each day and five days each week. It is important to take the needs of the "turnaround clock" into account when constructing the Turnaround Process. As with the Routine Maintenance Process, there are certain periods when high productivity is available and it is critical to capitalize on those periods. Conversely, there are periods when low productivity is possible (such as the midnight shift on Sunday night). It is best to minimize the workforce assigned to these periods and then to see that tasks are oriented toward "setting up" more productive periods.

The following critical issues concern the TAP clock:

- Nights are work shifts. Planning and organizing should be done on days. The night shift should follow the direction started on days rather than setting a different direction.
- Nights are less productive than days, and weekends are less productive than weekdays. Schedule critical path and near-critical path jobs on nights and weekends. Jobs that can be completed on a five day per week and daylight schedule should be scheduled for only. those periods.
- Provide additional skilled supervision at night to harvest as much productivity as possible.
- Management and Supervision needs to start earlier than their assigned crews. They need to be ready to put crews to work as soon as they arrive.
- The same need holds for people preparing safety permits, entry permits, welding permits, and other work permits. The permits need to be waiting on the crews rather than the opposite.

- All delays need to be escalated rapidly, independent of
  what shift they occur. If the people on duty can
  not make decisions to keep things moving,
  changes to the organization should be made.
  Delays cannot be accepted.
- "Gaps" need to be included in the schedule for work
  that cannot be done while large crews are present. Work like x-raying and hydro-blasting are
  better scheduled during these gaps.
- Consider the logistics of parking areas. The incoming
  shift cannot park in the same places as the leav-
  ing shift. There needs to be either a gap in the
  schedule or redundant parking spaces.
- Large meetings that take critical people away from the
  work area several times a day are interruptions.
  Keep meetings short. Involve only those who
  need to be involved. Hold the meetings on-site or
  within a short walk. Break meetings down into
  "systems". Assign "Systems Coordinators" so
  that attention can be focused on a limited area.
- Critical times are at the start of each shift (getting work
  started), around breaks (making sure people do
  not extend breaks), and at the end of the day
  (seeing people do not quit early). If supervisors
  are away from the workplace at important times,
  productivity will suffer.

In each of the above examples the objective is to identify
critical points on the TAP Clock and then develop ways to
address the possible problems. In many instances, the
solutions are based on providing extra supervision at critical times. Experience shows that simply adding supervisors may not solve the problem. Keep in mind that the

added supervisors:

- Need to be in the right places at the right times to recognize the problems.
- Need to know the problems they are expected to address.
- Need to know how to address the problem.
- Need to take action.

Everything else is meaningless unless people take action.

Process Descriptors

As with RMP, the key descriptors take the form of answers to the questions:

- Why
- What
- How
- Who
- When
- Where

To answer the question "why" we need to go to such extremes in planning and organizing turnarounds, think of it in these terms, "We are out-of-business while our money-making assets are down." Unlike the construction of a new facility, an turnaround typically involves an asset that has been a long-term part of the income stream. When it is out of service, none of the expenses associated with that asset is reduced, only the income stream. The objective is to restart the income stream as quickly as possible.

To answer the question "what", we need to address specifically what work will be done during the turnaround. The answer to that question is, the absolute minimum amount of work needed to achieve the premises. The premises should include:

- The desired run-length after the turnaround.
- The desired reliability after the turnaround.
- The desired efficiency during the next run.
- The desired thru-put and performance.
- The desired cost of the turnaround.

To answer the question "how" we need to understand some of our key objectives in performing the TAP.

1. One objective is that we conduct the process in a timely manner that allows for "optimization." Our objective should be to avoid completing preparations immediately ahead of the start of the turnaround, or after it has begun. Once the first pass schedule is completed there should be time to:

- Identify the critical path and near critical-path jobs.
- Re-plan critical-path and near critical-path jobs to reduce duration.
- Optimize the schedule to reduce the peak work-force and minimize off-shift work.

2. Another objective is to improve "scheduled-availability". Scheduled availability is the portion of time an asset is available to perform its intended function, based solely on scheduled events like turnarounds. The elements that control scheduled availability can only be addressed

while the asset is down. Two kinds of elements control scheduled availability:

- Run Limiters-The specific system(s) or device(s) that determine the maximum run-length between turnarounds.
- Duration Setters-The specific system(s) or device(s) that determine the critical path duration of the turnaround.

It should be the objective of each turnaround to identify run-limiter(s) and duration-setter(s) and see that they have been engineered to deliver the cost-effective optimum.

3. Another objective of a turnaround is to ensure that all improvements and enhancements are included. The list must include not only those improvements or enhancements that were identified during the past run, but also those that might be identified during the next run. All too often, runs are cut short to implement projects that require the unit to be shut down. That approach throws the whole annualized cost-effectiveness off schedule and dramatically increases annual costs. It is better to provide "tie-ins" for possible projects so that the plant can keep operating while connections are being made.

To answer the question "Who?", we need to understand the organization. Turnaround preparations are moderate-term or month-to-year time-frame operations. This kind of activity mixes poorly with day-to-day activities. So it is best to have some full time resources assigned. For larger turnaround activities it is best to have a full-time Turnaround Manager who is fully accountable for success. Depending on the size of the turnaround, the number of distinct system or units, and the physical distance between systems or units, it might also make sense to have one or more full time Systems Coordinators.

Managing full-time participants is not the difficult part of turnaround preparations. The difficult part has to do with individuals who have the needed expertise or knowledge but can only afford to participate on a part-time basis. This includes engineering technical experts (rotating equipment, electrical, instrument) and operating personnel. It is absolutely mandatory that these individuals contribute their knowledge and requirements at the right time, but they always seem to have something else to do.

Why do they need to contribute at the right time? They need to make their contribution at the proper time because so many tasks are sequential. For instance, you cannot optimize the plans and schedule until the comprehensive first-pass schedule is complete. In turn, you cannot complete the comprehensive first-pass schedule until all the detailed plans including work-force requirements and tasks have been determined through detailed planning. In turn, you cannot complete detailed plans and work-force requirements until the operating steps for shut-down, decontamination, and isolation are complete. Finally, you cannot create plans for shut-down, decontamination, and isolation, until the initial work scope is complete. In other words, you have to know what equipment will be out of use during the turnaround. When the TA Manager sends out a request for work-list items, even if it is eighteen months in advance, he needs people to cooperate by making their best effort to identify the work that must be completed during the turnaround. Delays in providing inputs will delay tasks that follow sequentially, and result in plans and schedules not being optimized.

The answer to the question "when" has been described in several of the sections above. One way of responding to "when" is by saying that turnaround preparations need to start earlier than most people think.

My experience is that I have found very few people who are good planners. In addition, even fewer individuals are good at "planning for planning". The question "How far in advance does it take to create a comprehensive plan?" is one that few people have had to answer. The companies and plants that are successful do not try to re-think the issue every time it surfaces. They simply have a system of procedures and protocols that trigger the start of preparations. Then they have a series of steps to be completed at specific times prior to the date of the TA to ensure success. For instance if an TA is to begin July 1, 2011, the TA Manager will be assigned on January 1, 2010 and he will set the schedule for completion of all tasks in the control document at the time he is first assigned.

The final descriptor is the question "where". It seems that this question becomes a larger issue with the passing of time.

In the past, one needed to think about the location of the unit or system being maintained during the turnaround and its location relative to shops, staging locations, and warehouses.

As turnarounds have grown over time, one must begin to consider:

- Parking for several thousand cars
- Transportation from remote parking areas
- Staging for acres of equipment and materials
- Logistics for getting remote parts and materials to the site.
- Location of qualified workforce. (How far will the crafts need to travel? Will you need to pay per diem to attract sufficient numbers?)
- Segregation of several contractors (If the overall job is too large for a single contractor, how will you segregate worksites, parking, material storage, etc.?)
- Are there contract issues? (Some contracts limit the distance a person can be expected to walk from the parking to the work site.)

Many plants have answered these questions over the years of their existence and simple follow historic patterns. New facilities have the benefit of needing to think through the best way to address them from the very start. Older facilities should think about how best to become "untracked". In other words, they should determine if the "way they have always done it" is the best way, or if it is time to break some old paradigms.

Details for Specific Steps

This section will provide a brief description of each of the process steps for the TAP.

"Identify TA Manager"

This step sounds simpler than it is. In identifying the TA Manager, the Plant Manager needs to "anoint" an individual to act with powers that are inconsistent with his position in the organization. The TA Manager needs to be granted sufficient powers to fulfill his accountability. Because this authority covers people from all organizations, it is only the Plant Manager or the Refinery Manager or the Shop Manager that can perform the ritual of "anointing". I use the term ritual because that is what it is. Leaders of all organizations need to be present when the Plant Manager says, "I have asked Joe Blow to act as the TA Manager for the XYZ turnaround. I expect that you and your organizations will provide your full cooperation and support."

"Identify TA Team"

Again, this is another step that may sound simpler than it really is. In many situations individuals view their names on a turnaround organization chart as a formality or space filler. Instead they need to understand that this identification implies their cooperation as described above.

If for some reason they cannot provide the support as described above, it is incumbent upon them to tell their supervisor and the TA Manager so that a change can be made _before_ things fall behind schedule.

"Adapt TA Calendar and Control Document"

Elsewhere in this book I have provided examples of a control document. Earlier in this chapter, I have provided an example of how to "back-calculate" the dates of the various tasks contained in the control document.

Once the initial control document is complete, a meeting of the entire TA Team should be scheduled and the tasks and timing of each task should be reviewed one-by-one. This is the opportunity for TA Team members to "Object now or forever hold your peace". In other words, if they do not object now, they will do their best to complete their assignments on time.

"Develop TA Premises"

In the past, many turnarounds were simply a repeat of what was done the last time... And the time before that, and the time before that, ad infinitum. That is a poor way to do business.

It is far better to develop a set of "turnaround premises" and create a current work-list that fulfills the premises. The turnaround premises identify the outcomes that are expected from the turnaround. The turnaround premises in effect identify the "boundaries" into which all aspects of the turnaround will fit.

The following is an example of a set of premises:

- After this turnaround the unit will be able to operate without outage for six years or until July 1, 2018.
- The efficiency of the unit will be restored to like-new standards (e.g. all exchangers will be cleaned).

- The production capacity of the unit will be returned to full capacity.
- The distilling capability and reaction capacity will be restored to like-new. (all trays cleaned and fixed bed catalysts restored).
- No spared equipment, or equipment that can be maintained while the unit is operating, will be worked during the Turnaround.
- The unit will be out of service no longer than five (5) weeks.
- The turnaround will include all work requiring a unit out age for the X, Y, and Z projects.
- Etc.

It is clear that some premises may appear to be in conflict. It is important then to determine which of the premises is controlling. For instance, it may be that all work cannot be done in five weeks. On the other hand, there may be severe economic penalties for exceeding five weeks, so that might be an absolute and other issues will need to work around that limitation.

"Assemble TA Work-list"

If all the steps up to this point have been done properly, this step should be easy. Just send out an e-mail to all the key contributors and wait for their input.

It normally is not that easy. There is typically someone who cannot seem to identify the required work in a timely manner. It will be necessary for the TA Manager to get the person's supervisor or ultimately the Plant Manager involved.

"Close TA Work-list"

Again, this is another one of those steps that may seem easier than it is.

It is mandatory that the work-list be "closed" on a specific date so that the following sequential steps can proceed. If work-list closure is viewed as a mere formality, people will continue to add work for the entire duration of TA preparation and execution. That activity will result in a lot of poorly-planned, poorly-scheduled and highly-disruptive work being done.

My experience has been that it is best to create a process for adding work after the "closure " date that is very "painful". The individual who identifies the work late should be expected to obtain approvals from the individuals who determine their salary and promotional opportunities, so that it becomes clear that proposing work after the clousure date is a bad thing.

"Initiate Cost Tracking/Forecasting System"

Fairly early in the turnaround process, costs start to mount. In order to collect all the costs associated with a turnaround, it is best to set up accounts early. That is the simple side of this TAP element.

The difficult side of this TAP element is that of cost "forecasting". Throughout TA preparation and execution it must be understood that the objective of the cost systems is to forecast the total cost at the end of the turnaround. The system needs to forecast what will be the total cost after all bills are in, all accounts are settled, and the TA is long since completed.

The turnaround cost consists of three components:
1. Spent
2. Committed
3. Remaining

Spent costs are the easy part. They have been already billed and possibly paid.

Committed costs are increasingly difficult. They are costs for labor, materials, rentals, supervision, staffing, etc that have already been consumed but have yet to be billed. The difficulty with this portion of costs comes from "timing". It is difficult to separate the end date for "spent costs" from the beginning date for "committed costs". It is even more difficult to separate the end-date for "committed costs" from the beginning date for "remaining costs".

For example, let's assume your turnaround has five major contractors on site and all five use different accounting systems. Assume that each of the five contractors has 500 employees on site.

Now assume that you like to update your forecast every Wednesday so you have asked the contractors to provide current information every Tuesday afternoon.
- One contractor may provide "Committed Costs" up to their last electronic billing date last Friday.
- One contractor may do the same, but they close their books on Saturday.
- Another contractor may use subcontractors who do not use electronic billing and are a month in arrears.

- Another contractor may provide information as of the last time they updated the critical-path schedule on Monday morning.
- The last contractor may be the only one to use information from an electronic gate count and provide exact information through Tuesday night.

The problem with these variations is that the inputs may cause you to under-estimate "committed costs" and under-forecast "Remaining Costs". If you are adjusting your forecasted costs based on productivity-to-date, and you are led to believe that you have accomplished current status with fewer resources than were actually required, you will assume you can finish the job with fewer resources than will be needed.

The last portion of the cost forecast is "Remaining Costs". As described in the last paragraph, the accuracy with which you track the resources already committed, and the work already completed (progress to date), is critical in projecting remaining costs.

Subtracting the completed work from total work tells you the amount of remaining work. In addition, determining how accurately you assessed past work will provide important insights into how accurate your remaining estimates are. If you under-estimated the number of man-hours needed to complete the past work, it is likely that the remaining work also has been underestimated. Your forecast then should be adjusted to account for the poor estimate.

In addition to the ability to address timing issues and estimating inaccuracy, the cost forecasting system needs to include two other features. Your budget should include allowances for:

- Contingency
- Addenda

Contingency funds are included for rain-outs, electrical storms, fires in adjacent plants, and other "Acts-of-God". If none of these occur, the entire amount set aside for contingencies should be returned at the end of the turnaround.

Addendum funds are intended to address scope growth, unknowns, added work, poor estimates etc. Each variance should be tracked separately so that future estimates can be adjusted accordingly. The Contingency and Addendum "draw-down" should be tracked and reported regularly so that management will know how likely it is that the turnaround will exceed budget, including allowances.

"Conduct Work List Review"

This review is a time consuming, but valuable step in the process. The work list review is an activity where key members of the TA Team are gathered together to review each and every work list item. The individual who identified each item is asked to present and "defend" it. Each item is compared to the turnaround premises. If it is within the boundaries created by the premises, the work item will be included in the turnaround. If not, it will be excluded.

All future items recommended through the "work-add" system will be exposed to the same scrutiny, making it impossible to circumvent the review process.

"Order Long-Lead Materials"

One of the benefits of having an experienced TA Manager is the ability to look at a work-list and understand what parts and materials need to be ordered early.

Some materials take longer to be delivered because they require some engineering or development. Some have complicated fabrication steps. Increasingly, special alloys take longer to find. In any project, there are occasions when material availability can become an problem.

"Conduct Detailed Planning"

As one reviews a work-list for a turnaround, there are a myriad of simple jobs that do not require special planning. Conversely, there are always a few jobs that require more detailed planning. Preparation for these latter jobs will benefit from starting early.

One example I recall involved removing a brick refractory system that was backed up with asbestos insulation from a large vessel in a refinery unit. The specific refinery had two duplicate units, both containing similar vessels with the same archaic refractory/insulation system.

One unit experienced a brick fall and needed to go into an emergency shutdown. The brick refractory and asbestos was removed and replaced with gunnite without benefit of detailed planning in advance. The labor portion of removing the brick refractory and asbestos amounted to more than a million dollars.

When the same refractory/insulation replacement job was planned and executed on the "twin unit" a year later, with the benefit of advanced detailed planning, the brick and asbestos removal was completed using robotic devices that minimized human involvement. In addition to being a safer and cleaner job, it cost less than $20,000.

The lesson is that it is possible to "work smart" when there is an opportunity to examine all the alternatives.

"Develop Release Bid Packages"

It is best to organize your work-force as early as possible. One way to organize your work-force is to force yourself to divide all the work being done into packages and bid the work.

This step not only secures a commitment for the resources needed to complete the work, it signals the surrounding industrial community that you are planning a turnaround at that time. They should avoid conflicting projects during that time, or risk creating a work-force shortage.

"Integrate Capital Projects"

The integration of capital projects into turnarounds has always been a real pain. Typically capital project managers develop plans and schedules in a much less detailed manner than is required for turnarounds. During a typical project a high-level schedule is developed before starting, and detailed plans and schedules are created only during the day or, at most, the week before execution.

All work for a turnaround, including all capital work, needs to be completely planned and scheduled before the turnaround begins. There is no time to plan work or create a schedule during a turnaround. During a turnaround you do two things:

1. Execute already planned and scheduled work.
2. Plan and dovetail new work found during the turnaround into the existing schedule. This work should only be something that was absolutely impossible to identify before the turnaround.

My recommendation is for all project work to be turned over to the TA Manager for accomplishment. All project work done during a turnaround must be planned in the same manner, and to the same level of detail, as other TA work.

"Develop Shut-down (SD) and Start Up (SU) Plans"

It is not unusual for operations personnel to say they have files of past operating procedures for shutdown and start up and there is no value in these being updated.

However, the premises and the work-scope changes for every turnaround. Therefore if you are using the same SD and SU plans as were used for past turnarounds you are causing inefficiency. You are either shutting down and starting up (and decontaminating and isolating) systems that will not be worked, or you are not preparing systems that will be worked. In either event, the result will be inefficiency.

"Develop A Cost Estimate"

Once the entire scope of work is well known, it is best to develop an accurate cost estimate as soon as possible. This step is intended to avoid "sticker shock" at a point when it is too late to make changes. If the cost estimate is developed too late, and you are asked to reduce the cost by removing work, it may result in the schedule being left looking pretty "ragged". Again, the result is lost efficiency.

"Create A Comprehensive Schedule"

The same situation is true of the overall TA schedule. It is best to be early, to avoid surprises when it is too late to make changes. Then, if there is a need to make the TA shorter in duration, you can do so in an intelligent, organized fashion.

It might seem that you should be able to simply "push the button" and have your critical path scheduling software produce a schedule, but that seldom happens. Several weeks might be required between the first time the button is pushed and the point at which the final schedule is produced. It is important to track the critical-path and near-critical-path steps through from beginning to end. In many projects, the sequencing of activities does not occur as might be envisioned.

In a fairly complicated example of what can go wrong, I once found a situation where the scheduling program provided a misleading duration.

In this situation, the critical path for a major turnaround involved a distilling column that was being modified to increase the number of trays. Two contractors were involved in the critical path work. One was a specialty contractor who would remove the old trays, modify the column by installing new nozzles and supports, then install the new trays. The second firm was a piping contractor who would install revised piping to all the new tray connections.

I will try to simplify the details of this problem. Because there were two contractors performing different parts of the job, the managing contractor allowed them to plan and organize their work separately. In preparing the schedule, the managing contractor used a number of "dummy tasks" in the schedule to represent the work being done in the column, so that external piping work could be scheduled before planning the internal work.

After the initial schedules were produced by the scheduling software, it was found that the critical duration seemed to be insensitive to changes in tasks and sequencing of tasks around the column.

A detailed analysis of the schedule showed that the dummy tasks had not been removed. When the tasks representing installation of trays were included, they were tied to the same starting points as the dummy tasks but not to the ending points. As a result, the dummy tasks continued to determine the turnaround duration. Because the dummy tasks were left in place, the program continued to run and calculate a duration, so the problem was not apparent.

Without digging through several thousand tasks and performing a logic check, the problem would never have been found. This problem might seem like an extreme example, but it is not unusual. Whenever there is more than one contractor contributing to a schedule, and more than one person inputting and sequencing tasks, problems are possible.

As a result, it is a good idea to take the time needed to review the schedule in detail and to re-run the program several times to see if you get the results that you expect.

"Assemble Work Packages"

At this point, it is a good idea to think about how work gets done during a major turnaround. Everyday tens, if not hundreds of new jobs get started. Often, those jobs are being supervised by someone you do not know, and being done by someone new to your plant. Think about what you want to tell them and what is needed to ensure that each of those jobs gets done effectively and efficiently. It is best to hand the supervisor a work package containing:

• Possibly a map of the plant so they can find where the work is located.

- Possibly a picture of the equipment involved showing how it looks now.
- Possibly the same picture marked up to show how it will look when completed.
- A list of tools needed to do the job.
- A list of all parts and materials needed to do the job and where they are located.
- Possibly a map of the lay-down yard showing where materials are staged.
- A description of the steps involved in performing the work.
- Any specifications that must be met in performing the work.
- Any inspection points or "hold points" where work must be inspected before proceeding.
- Any permits required to perform the work.
- Any special safety equipment.
- Sign-offs needed to confirm that the work is completed.

"Conduct A Management Review"

Another "ritual" that should take place after preparations are substantially complete but still several months prior to a turnaround is a formal management review. This review provides an opportunity for the TA Manager to explain all the details of the TA to both plant and corporate senior managers.

A key feature of this review is the opportunity to present "risks" and "concerns". It is an opportunity for the TA team to have management "share" knowledge of the risks associated with scope, schedule, and budget limitations.

"Optimize Schedule and Job Plans"

Once the "first-pass" schedule and plans for individual jobs have been completed, hopefully there is still time to go through an optimization step.

Frenquently your critical path schedule will follow the pattern shown below.

With this pattern, there is one job that forms the critical-path duration for the turnaround. After the critical-path sequence, there are a number of "near-critical-path" jobs. Finally, there are a large number of jobs that are much shorter than the critical-path duration.

Job Duration ®

When optimizing the schedule, first look at the critical path job. Is there a way to significantly reduce its duration? For example, if the critical path duration is the result of a large amount of repair work being done during the turnaround, is it possible to move a portion of that work out of the turnaround (maybe by doing some pre-fabrication).

Developing some creative approach may reduce the critical-path duration of the longest job.

After that reduction, a number of jobs may become grouped. Once that happens, it is necessary to reduce the critical path duration of several jobs to reduce the duration of the turnaround. There are two things to keep in mind at this point:

1. The combined cost of reducing all the competing " near-critical-path" jobs must be offset by the value of getting the unit back early.
2. If any of the techniques being used to reduce duration are risky, it is possible to spend a lot of money and effort and obtain no return if any of the strategies fails.

Apart from reducing the turnaround duration, the optimization step should include minimizing off-shift work and balancing work-force levels.

"Release Purchase Orders and Rentals"

Purchase orders for normal-lead-time materials, and for rentals of readily-available tools and equipment, should be released several months prior to the turnaround. There seldom are "surprises" in this area, but occasionally you will find that options typically taken for granted have changed. Occasionally, rentals for mobile equipment, particularly large cranes, produce unexpected excitement close to the turnaround.

"Assemble An Execution Team"

During particularly large turnarounds it is advisable to leverage your inherent knowledge of the plant and its systems by using plant personnel to coordinate the activities of contractors. Crafts can add more by acting as temporary foremen or contractor coordinators than they can by simply working as wrench-turners.

"Complete Field Staging"

Within the month or so prior to the turnaround it is time to bring in temporary trailers and tool rooms, stage lay-down yards, and outhouses, etc. This work again is better early than late. Done early, you will learn about obstructions and inconveniences while there is still time to correct them.

When laying things out, keep in mind that time spent wandering around lost is time that is wasted. Create and post maps of key facilities so that people can quickly find them. One approach that seems to work well is to mark off lay-down yards using an alpha-numeric grid. This will help people quickly find the materials they are seeking.

When laying out your laydown yard be sure to provide roads wide enough for stake trucks, cranes and fork lifts. Provide readily visible "street signs" at frequent intervals

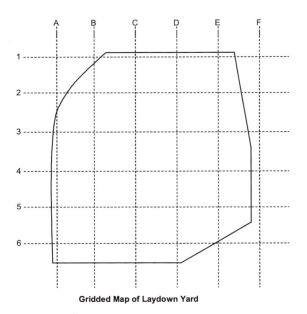

Gridded Map of Laydown Yard

so that people can easily find locations of material. Be sure to keep your "map" up to date as materials are set out. Also, be sure to keep like items together so that people do not have to wonder all over looking for pieces of the same type of equipment.

"Initiate Work Add System"

Several months prior to a major turnaround you should initiate the works add system. There are several rules for an effective works add system:

1. Include proper approvals.
2. Use the same premises that were used to approve the basic work-scope.

3 Make it "painful" to add work that could have been
   identified earlier.

"Begin Tracking Schedule and Costs"

In the weeks before the turnaround it is critical that you
begin using the system that will be used during the turnaround to track schedule and costs. The objective is to
"wring-out" the system before things get busy. If contractors cannot seem to get job-status reports or work-force
spending sheets in on-time during staging, it is unlikely
they will do so during the turnaround. Find out if there is
a problem early.

"Begin Tracking Key Measures"

It is critical to begin calculating, posting, and discussing
Key Measures long before the turnaround. If there is
something missing, or if the system is not designed correctly, fix the problem before the turnaround.

All the effort associated with Key Measures is intended to
produce an effect. These efforts are not just for wall
paper. If appropriate individuals are not paying attention
or are not taking corrective actions, it is better to find out
and correct these problems before the turnaround
begins.

"Complete Turnaround"

If everything has been done as described above, this will
be the easy part.

Said differently, all the preparations should allow you to manage the vast majority of the turnaround "by objectives". Only a small portion of the turnaround will need to be managed "by exception". Rather than waking up in a new world every day, this result should reduce the frequency to maybe once per week.

"Critique Turnaround"

A critique of the turnaround is not simply determining what went well and what went badly. If you have a clearly-defined Turnaround Process, you should be able to determine what was accomplished according to the TAP and what was not completed.

If work was done in accordance with the process and was not successful, change the process. If the work was not done according to the process, change the behaviors of the participants.

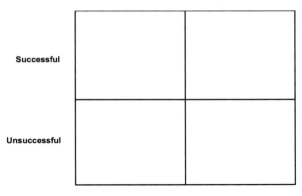

Accountability – Responsibility – Matrix

The format of an Accountability-Responsibility-Matrix (ARM) was included in the RMP chapter. Each key role in a turnaround organization should be included in the turnaround ARM. A key point to keep in mind is that during a turnaround, contractor employees may fill key roles. If they do, three points should be kept in mind:

1. The contractors need to be provided with training on their roles.
2. Contact employees in key roles may not understand the concept of accountability or responsibility. That concept needs to be included in the training.

3. Contract employees may not be able to execute accountabilities when dealing with employees of the owner. They frequently view owner employees as their "boss". Accountabilities often call for the contractor to act as the "boss" of the owner's employees. (Although the contractor employees will never be able to deliver the desired results, the contractor will never admit to that fact. That admission would interfere with the contractor's ability to sell man-hours.)

Roles for Each Individual Involved

Again, the RMP chapter provided an example of a role description that was developed from the items in the ARM.

The same comments as described above apply to the

role descriptions. It is important not only to develop a set of role descriptions for all the positions in your turnaround organization, but to review the roles for practicality.

During a large turnaround, it is not uncommon to use individuals in roles for which they are only marginally qualified. Using a carpenter to lead a scaffolding crew, or an operator to lead a blinding crew, may stretch those individuals into uncomfortable areas. But those kinds of assignments are likely to be successful with the right preparation.

On the other hand, using a contractor to lead an activity like scope development is not as likely to be successful. In this position, you are asking a person to complete a task that is very much shaded by his ability to exert influence in an area where he has no influence. Unless the person has unusual charisma, he will not be successful. (If he has that much charisma, he is probably out selling time-shares).

Instructions for Using IT Systems

The principal IT system used to organize a turnaround is the scheduling software. It would be possible to devote an entire book to turnaround scheduling and software. Rather than taking that approach I will describe the system that has worked best for me.

First, the way the scheduling system is used must complement the planning system. All information is stored in one place only, and all functions are completed only once.

Let's start by describing the planning system. The planning system consists of a duplicate set of manila folders containing all the information described earlier under the "Assemble Work Packages" portion of the "Details for Specific Steps" section in this chapter. A set of manila folders should be prepared for every job of the turnaround. Each folder should be identified with a code that will help you to find it later, and it helps if the system identifies where the work is located and the kind of work it covers. For instance, a folder containing machinist work in the fractionation section of a crude unit might be coded CR-FR-MA-001. The job in the folder has probably been broken down into a number of tasks. The individual tasks can be labeled with individual numbers or letters (e.g. CR-FR-MA-001a).

All these folders are then stored in the sequential order in which they will be accomplished, either in filing cabinets or cardboard boxes.

The scheduling system will be constructed with information from each of these tasks. Rather than long verbal descriptions, the code describing the task and a short title can be input into the critical-path planning program, along with crew size and duration. This approach minimizes the amount of extraneous information. Once sequencing information (predecessors and successors) has been input, it will be possible to run the schedule and produce a critical-path plan that is as simple and easy to use as possible.

During the turnaround, the scheduling program will be used like a "call-file". When a task is identified by the program for accomplishment, the scheduler goes to the file containing the work package and removes one copy of the file. This copy is given to the appropriate planner or system coordinator, who will in turn assign it to the appropriate field foreman.

An important consideration in using a critical-path scheduling program is the issue of "too little" versus "too much". It is not uncommon for plants to vacillate between entering minute tasks in the CPM program and entering large tasks in the program. Tasks that are too small make the system cumbersome and difficult to maintain. Tasks that are too large make the output meaningless. My experience is that the balance afforded by using work-packs to contain details and the scheduling program to contain sequence and work-force levels provides best results.

Characteristics of the Turnaround Process

Adapting Individual Schedules to the TA Process Requirements

Many, if not most, of the people involved in a turnaround are stepping out of their normal roles when working on the turnaround. When people temporarily fulfill a role that is different from their norm, they frequently attempt to continue some of the old patterns to make their new role seem more normal. In other words, people continue to want to work in their own "comfort zone".

In some jobs that may work, but in many it will not. If a person is allowed to continue using his normal office, attending normal meetings, reviewing all normal reports, it will be difficult to create a truly efficient and effective turnaround pattern.

It is better to have the turnaround team move into temporary turnaround quarters and to create a schedule that breaks old norms.

In order to keep the turnaround preparations on schedule, and to ensure that adequate attention is being paid, it is best to get the participants focused 100% on turnaround activities.

Integration with Customer Needs

Earlier we discussed setting turnaround premises as a basis for the overall turnaround plan. For the most part, these premises are set by the customer. It is the role of the TA Manager and TA Team to "facilitate" premise setting. But, the customer determines the premises.

Later in the chapter on the Project Management Process, we will discuss setting requirements for projects. Briefly, all requirements fit into one of three categories for any significant effort including both projects and turnarounds:

- Scope
- Schedule
- Budget

Customer premises for the length of the run after the turnaround, reliability, availability, and efficiency will ultimately determine the scope of work. Customer premises for the maximum period the plant can be out of service will ultimately determine the schedule. Customer premises for financial performance will determine the budget. Although customers can identify premises that shape all three categories of requirements, they cannot identify premises that are in conflict. Scope, Schedule, and Budget are interdependent, so it is important that they are consistent with one another. If they are inconsistent, it is important to highlight that fact to the customer as early in the turnaround preparation phase as is possible.

Integration with Support Functions

Each and every support function in the plant should be asked to provide a TA Team member. Some members of the TA Team will be full-time, and others will be part-time. Each member should be invited to participate in all TA Team Meetings. The needs of each of the support organizations should be represented by their member of the TA Team.

Leaning Out the End Product

Of all the activities conducted within a plant, a turnaround is most susceptible to waste so there is the greatest opportunity to eliminate waste.

The following is a list of reasons why waste exists:

1. People have the attitude. "While the unit is out of service, I never want to see a time when work is not proceeding."
2. Weekends and off-shifts are poorly supervised. There are more hiding places after dark.

3. Contractor employees have no loyalty to the owner.
4. Few plants are well equipped to handle a large influx of people.
5. Many areas have insufficient numbers of skilled crafts to handle a large TA, so many contractor employees are barbers, cooks and …
6. Many of the individuals acting as supervisors on large TA's are typically craftspeople. They have little supervisory experience or skills.
7. And on, and on.

The following is a list of ways to eliminate waste.

1. Implement incentive contracts that encourage productivity.
2. Walk the job frequently. Identify unproductive areas. See that contractor management takes corrective action and has regular lay-offs of unproductive personnel.
3. Conduct regular job-delay surveys. Identify areas like "waiting for tools" or "waiting for permits" where improvements can be made and action taken.
4. Monitor schedule productivity (planned man-hours divided by actual man-hours). Provide additional scrutiny to areas where productivity is different from other areas. (P/A may be high or it might be low, but it should be similar in all parts of the project.)
5. Keep your eye on trash bins and dumpsters to see if good materials or recyclable materials are being discarded.

6. Manage rentals closely. Bring them into the plant only when needed. Release them as soon as they are no longer needed. Don't wait for the end of the turn-around to return all rentals.

7. And so on, and so on.

Discipline

Turnarounds frequently entail assembling a group of experienced and highly successful employees to manage portions of the activity.

An unfortunate feature in using successful and strong-willed individuals is that they like to do things their own way. Unfortunately, that practice will lead to problems. Participants need to follow established procedures because they set the basis for interactions. When people "do it their own way", systems will break down.

Frequently it is better to use a weaker individual who will function within the system and as a part of the team, than a stronger individual who will free-lance.

Evergreen

A critique should be conducted at the conclusion of every turnaround.

The objective of performing the critique is more than identifying what went wrong. It should identify situations that went wrong because TAP procedures were not followed. It should also identify situations that went wrong despite or because TAP procedures were followed.

If the TAP procedures led to poor results, the procedures need to be changed.

Mechanism for Feeding Entropy

Each and every work management process needs a "process owner" and the Turnaround Process is no exception. This individual should understand the process and how it is intended that each element be handled. This individual should have the time, resources, and authority to ensure that the TAP is being followed as designed and intended.

If the TAP is not being followed, the TAP process owner should be held accountable for taking whatever corrective actions are needed.

Additional Thoughts from References

Levitt, Joel; *Managing Maintenance Shutdowns and Outages;* Industrial Press, New York, 2004

As mentioned in the Introduction, the objective of the Little Black Book of Maintenance Excellence is to provide a comprehensive yet high-level description of all the significant elements of Maintenance Excellence. As such, the reader is directed to more detailed texts on specific subjects if he is interested in learning more. This referenced text provides excellence details concerning turnaround planning and execution.

Once an organization has introduced the discipline needed to begin preparations early enough to make a difference, the next step is to use that time effectively to create thorough plans for all the tasks, then to combine all the plans into a comprehensive schedule.

When that schedule is complete and the turnaround begins, it is time to "work your plan". In the referenced text, the author provides useful insights into activities needed to assemble detailed plans, assemble those plans into a comprehensive schedule, and then use the schedule to manage the outage.

Womack, James P. and Jones, Daniel T., *Lean Thinking,* Simon & Schuster, New York, 1996

Turnarounds are often viewed as situations where it makes sense to "throw money at a problem" to solve it. As a result, they often provide the greatest opportunities for eliminating waste. Once the Turnaround Process (TAP) is well organized and disciplined, the opportunity to recognize waste is enhanced. The referenced text will provide the reader with the knowledge needed to capture that opportunity and eliminate TAP-related waste.

CHAPTER 6
THE PROGRAM MANAGEMENT PROCESS

The future has a way of arriving unannounced.
George Will

I recall a discussion I had with a respected friend some years ago. We were talking about the performance of a particularly successful individual and my friend said that the person was viewed as being able to make good choices concerning risks. Specifically, he was known for being able to defer or reduce work without suffering the consequences.

After this discussion, I thought for a long time about the observation my friend made concerning this individual. Specifically, what talent was being recognized?

- Was this individual able to identify situations where everyone else overestimated the risk of failure?
- Was he able to be successful because he knew that reducing the amount of work being done would not increase the risk of failure to a significant level?
- Was this individual a lot smarter than others so that he could quickly calculate risk, while others had to operate on gut-feelings only?

- Or was he just lucky?
- Or was he willing to accept risks that others were not?
- Or did he know he would never remain in a single position long enough to suffer the consequences of his poor choices?

Despite how this specific individual achieved success, most of us go about life with the confidence that nature is forgiving, and we will always get a second chance. As a result, it is not uncommon for people to make poor choices and depend on a forgiving nature. Forgiveness may simply be a matter of the dice we have set in play, rolling "snake eyes" only after we have had a chance to re-think and re-position ourselves. Or it may be that the resulting failure happens only after we have moved on to another position.

Much of a plant or shop's infrastructure is maintained using medium to long term programs. In the Program Management Process (PMP), our choices always determine the level of risk. Wise choices reduce the risk of failure, or at least save resources without increasing risk to unacceptable levels. Poor choices increase risk to the point that the value of the risk is greater than the associated savings.

In some situations we have an opportunity to recover from poor choices before the risk pays out (in other words, before the failure occurs). In others, the failure occurs early in the statistical failure interval and an unkind nature makes us pay for our unwise choice. In still other instances, we get ourselves into a bind. We make a choice that is irreversible and we have no alternative than to live with the poor results.

In using the term "irreversible choice" I am referring to a situation where it is impossible to return to the earlier status and simply start doing what was stopped. An example is not changing the oil in your car for 50,000 miles. Simply resuming regular oil changes will not undo the damage that occurred during the period of neglect. Resetting the clock will require an engine overhaul.

Considering all the different issues described above, it should be clear that there are right ways to manage work using programs, and there are wrong ways. This chapter is dedicated to the elements that should be addressed when developing and managing maintenance programs. By maintenance programs, I am referring to those regular programs like painting, insulation maintenance, and maintenance of structural fireproofing.

The elements that should be considered include:
1. The investment model that compares alternative approaches.
2. The program process used for identifying and managing work.
3. The system for prioritizing work.
4. Development and implementation methods.

Background

One of the most common activities handled as a program is the exterior painting program for a plant. The paint program is a good example that includes all the elements that should be considered. These elements include balancing risks and costs of not performing the work with the costs associated with a well-organized and well-managed program. It also provides an example of a situation that can be viewed as an irreversible choice.

In a plant, particularly a plant containing hazardous or toxic substances in a corrosive environment (like the Gulf coast of the US), the decision to paint or not to paint has less to do with aesthetics than with equipment integrity and safety.

Few companies spend money to "get ahead" of their painting needs. With that thought in mind, let's assume that an optimum paint program is one that applies paint at exactly the right time or shortly before the coating system will fail if not maintained. A good coating system is capable of several years of life, so there are several years between maintenance cycles on each part of the facility. Rather than painting the entire plant one year, then waiting several years before returning to paint the entire plant again, the plant is divided into a number of near-equal segments, in which paint is applied at exactly the right time every several years.

This optimum program is designed to function in this manner for a variety of reasons:

- It keeps this part of the budget constant. Bean counters like consistent budgets.

- It uses consistent coating systems so that everyone knows how the system works and how long it is supposed to last. Even someone who is not a "paint expert" can identify areas that are not per forming as expected.
- Painting can be done in good weather. Paint contractors can then employ consistent, experienced crews.
- Staying on schedule prevents coating failures.

Now let's assume that someone gets the bright idea to cut funds from the paint program. When funds for the paint program are cut, and the regular maintenance of coating systems is interrupted, appearance is the least important thing to suffer. Assuming that we are running a truly "optimized" program, and we are harvesting all the available life from the coating system, as soon as we stop the program, the coating system will begin to suffer adverse effects.

Let's discuss these effects in increasing order of importance:

1. If re-coated on schedule, surfaces will require a minimal amount of surface preparation. If coating system integrity is lost, abrasive blasting or other forms of surface preparation will be needed.
2. Once the coating system fails, surface metal loss will begin to occur. In places where metal loss (corrosion) has occurred, abrasive blasting is definitely required. Weld build-up or component replacement may be required if damage is severe.
3. The organization of the overall program quickly

becomes "irreversible" Because you cannot return to the earlier annual program. You have to play catch-up. That means you will need to use a larger crew and personnel that are new to the plant, which adds risk. (I recall a situation in which an inexperienced laborer working for a paint contractor triggered the overspeed trip on the feed pump for a major unit with a broom while sweeping abrasive residue. The resulting mess shut the unit down, and the subsequent restart attempt caused damage requiring an extended unit shutdown.)

4. If metal loss goes undetected and proceeds to the point of causing a leak, either a safety event (fire or explosion), or an environmental event (toxic release), can result. As compared to all other results, these accidents can be the most significant because it is unclear where the effects will end.

The Investment Model

A basic premise of the program process is that a cost-effective, proactive maintenance program for painting, insulation, fire proofing, cathodic protection, and other similar activities can prevent all the following outcomes:

• Repeated extensive surface preparation
• Extensive metal loss due to external corrosion
• Reactive repairs due to external corrosion
• Expensive and sophisticated inspection techniques necessitated by external corrosion
• Unacceptable deterioration in appearance due to coat-

ing and insulation deterioration
- Undesired releases of hazardous or toxic materials,
  resulting in safety or environmental events.

The useful life of equipment and structure need not be limited by external corrosion. Proper maintenance of protective systems is a more cost-effective strategy for managing external deterioration than reactive inspection and repairs of damage.

Two Models for Investing

There are two extremes that can be used to describe the alternative approaches of investing in plant infrastructure.

The first is the highly-reactive approach described in Table 1, which describes the situation where for every dollar spent on painting-related activities:

- Five cents or less is spent on proactive maintenance of
  systems before deterioration has occurred.
- Forty-five to fifty cents is spent on more sophisticated
  inspection programs, repairs to lost metal,
  and other related activities that are required after
  significant deterioration has occurred (but not
  specifically related to a leak).
- Nominally thirty cents is spent on unscheduled leak
  repairs. This expenditure includes the cost of
  repairing the leak, losses to unit capacity, lost
  product, and administrative costs associated with
  safety or environmental incidents.
- Finally, nominally 20 cents is spent on costs associated with unscheduled shutdowns for repairs. This

amount includes fixed costs, variable costs, and lost profit, associated with the unit being shut down to repair a leak resulting from external corrosion.

Table 1

	Coating System and External Corrosion Management			
	Portion of Each Dollar Spent			
Proactive Coating and Insulation Program	Reactive External Corrosion and Metal Integrity Inspection Program	Repair and Response to Unexpected Leaks	Unscheduled Shutdowns to Repair Leaks	Total
1A	1B	1C	1D	
Approve Budget	Inspect for Metal Loss	Install Clamps on Leaks	Repair / Replacement	
Inspect Coatings and Insulation Visually	Identify Needed Repairs	Repair/Replace Leaking Components	Unit Capacity Impact	
Identify Needed Work	Schedule Repair/Replacement	HS&E Incidents		
Plan Work	Record Keeping	Unit Capacity Impact		
Schedule Work	Reactive Painting	Leak Repair Cost		
Execute Work	Follow Up	Lost Production		
Follow Up	Re-Inspection			
$.00 to $.05	$.45 to $.50	$0.30	$0.20	$1.00

The second approach is the highly proactive approach described in Table 2. In this approach, only thirty cents is

Table 2

	Proactive Coating and Insulation Program	Reactive External Corrosion and Metal Integrity Inspection Program	Repair and Response to Unexpected Leaks	Unscheduled Shutdowns to Repair Leaks	Total
	2A	2B	2C	2D	
Coating System and External Corrosion Management — Portion of Each Dollar Spent	Approve Budget	Inspect for Metal Loss	Install Clamps on Leaks	Repair / Replacement	
	Inspect Coatings and Insulation Visually	Identify Needed Repairs	Repair/Replace Leaking Components	Unit Capacity Impact	
	Identify Needed Work	Schedule Repair/Replacement	HS&E Incidents		
	Plan Work	Record Keeping	Unit Capacity Impact		
	Schedule Work	Reactive Painting	Leak Repair Cost		
	Execute Work	Follow Up	Lost Production		
	Follow Up	Re-Inspection			
	$0.25		<------ $.05 ------>		$0.30

spent for every dollar that is spent in the reactive approach. Of that thirty cents, twenty-five cents is spent on a pro-active paint program and only five cents is spent on the undesired results of uncontrolled deterioration.

In the pro-active approach, investment is made in avoiding problems rather than dealing with problems after they occur.

Comparing the two approaches, five times the money needs to be spent on pro-active painting to reduce costs and eliminate negative consequences. Plants that are currently spending very little on pro-active programs can expect an initial "bulge" in spending until they get caught up and can fall back to normal maintenance levels.

Transforming from Approach 1 to Approach 2

Although the economics of these two approaches seem almost "intuitively obvious", many plants choose not to practice maintenance in a manner consistent with the second approach. The reason is that there is no obvious point where paint (or other similar systems), fails. If there was, it would be easy to say, "We need to fix it right now" and money could easily be justified. Since there is no clear point of failure, funds associated with these programs are frequently the first to be cut from the budget. Seldom does anyone take the time to quantify the ultimate costs of making those cuts.

The first step in "forcing" the transition from approach 1 to approach 2 is to collect data on all costs shown in Table

1. These costs include both expense (fixed costs and variable costs), capital (capital costs associated with replacement of major assets resulting from exterior deterioration), and lost profit.

The second step is to calculate and budget funds to upgrade the programs to the pro-active approach. The amount that should be budgeted is described in the following equation, where symbols (2A, 1A, 1B, 1C, 1D) are totals from the elements included in the columns shown in Table 1 and Table 2.

$$2A = 1A + 25\% \text{ of } (1B + 1C + 1D)$$

It is important to recognize that the objective of the proactive approach is to bias spending toward pro-activity using a portion of the costs of metal deterioration and negative consequences. Clearly, there is a practical limit to this approach. If 1C and 1D includes the effects associated with a major event, it would be possible to drive recommended spending well beyond a practical amount.

It is also important to recognize that as the amount being spent for categories 1B, 1C and 1D decrease, the spending for 2A will also decrease. The enterprise then begins to benefit from being proactive.

The Program Process

The following flow chart shows the process that is used to identify, justify, and accomplish the work in a well-organized program process.

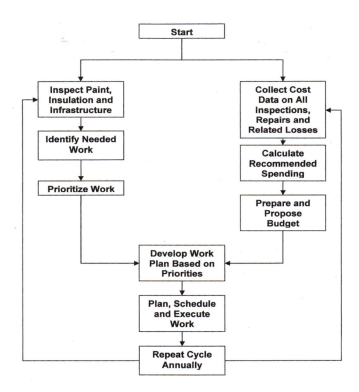

The Prioritization System

Four characteristics are used to prioritize work done as part of programs on plant infrastructure.

The first and most direct is when the work is on a vessel or is on piping that contains material capable of causing a problem if released. Here the issue is volume. Large vessels contain more material than piping systems, so risks associated with failure are far greater. In turn deterioration to purely structural components creates a lower risk. This lower risk continues until the components have deteriorated to the point of collapse, or unless the structure is supporting a vessel or piping containing hazardous materials. In those conditions, priority should be adjusted to ensure timely maintenance.

The second characteristic is "service class". Service class definitions can be defined in a manner that is consistent with standards (like API 570), or regulatory guidelines. Following is an example of classes:

- Class 1 - Service with the highest potential of resulting in an immediate safety or environmental incident if a leak were to occur. (e.g. likely to vaporize upon release)
- Class 2 – Services not included in Class 1 but within the battery limits of a process plant and selected off-site systems.
- Class 3 – Services that are flammable but do not readily vaporize when they leak and are not in high-activity areas.
- Class 4 – Utility services carrying such materials as steam, condensate, nitrogen, etc.

The third characteristic is "suspect area". This characteristic is either "yes" or "no" based on a visual survey of the specific system and its location, for the likelihood of external corrosion or other possible forms of deterioration.

- Highly suspect areas include painted or insulated areas exposed to water mist, steam vents, or other

> sources of moisture. Insulated surfaces exhibiting algae growth or water dripping would also be considered suspect.
> • Configuration is also an important consideration. Small-diameter piping with many fittings, screwed piping, and point contacts, are susceptible to concentration cell corrosion.

The fourth characteristic is "condition code". Condition codes for paint and insulation systems are described in Table 3 on the next page.

Once all the above characteristics have been determined for all the systems being considered for work, it is possible to determine the relative priority of each area of work. Table 4 provides a relative priority system that can be used. For systems not listed (like structure, fireproofing, and cathodic protection), it will be necessary to identify appropriate characteristics and then place them in the appropriate rank by priority level.

Program Development and Implementation

Another of the significant premises to this approach is that the program can be conducted in a manner that results in optimum cost and value. Clearly if we apply techniques that allow us to pro-actively identify the need for work, we can take maximum advantage of the opportunity to thoroughly plan and tightly schedule work in advance.

The following points describe additional features of work that is completed using the program process:

Table 3

Condition Code	Painted Surface Condition Description	Insulation System Condition Description
1	Undamaged or Cosmetic Deterioration Only	Undamaged or Cosmetic Deterioration Only
2	Minor Deterioration	Caulk and/or Weather Jacket Needs Repair
3	Significant Deterioration of Coating	Damaged Jacket of Insulation, Repair Required
4	Minor Metal Loss	Wet, Exposed Inslation, Need to Strip and Inspect.
5	Significant Metal Loss	Known Metal Loss

Table 4

Priority For Paint and Insulation Repair Activities

Priority Order	Paint or Insulation	Class	Suspect Area	Fixed Equipment or Piping
1	Insulation	1	Yes	F.E.
2	Paint	1	Yes	F.E.
3	Insulation	1	Yes	Piping
4	Paint	1	Yes	Piping
5	Insulation	2,3,4	Yes	F.E.
6	Paint	2,3,4	Yes	F.E.
7	Insulation	2,3,4	Yes	Piping
8	Paint	2,3,4	Yes	Piping
9	Insulation	1	No	F.E.
10	Paint	1	No	F.E.
11	Insulation	1	No	Piping
12	Paint	1	No	Piping
13	Insulation	2,3,4	No	F.E.
14	Paint	2,3,4	No	F.E.
15	Insulation	2,3,4	No	Piping
16	Paint	2,3,4	No	Piping

- Before starting work, the scope can be pre-defined. Throughout, the definition can tightly control the amount of work that is completed and the resources that are committed.

- If contracted, it can be bid and released on a fixed-price basis. If some things are hidden during bidding, those areas should be uncovered as quickly as possible at the start of the job, and a fixed price estimate prepared. This procedure gives the owner the option of changing direction.

- Bids can be competitive and all-inclusive. The proposal should include prep work, scaffolding, trans portation, clean-up, and disposal. If materials are included, requirements must be clearly specified so that an apples-to-apples comparison can be made.

- Work should be warranted, then the warranty enforced if there are problems.

- A specific individual can be set up to monitor quality, schedule, and monitor administrative issues. The individual should be adequately familiar with the work being done.

Additional Thoughts from References

Lamb, Richard G., Availability Engineering & Management for Manufacturing Plant Performance, Prentice-Hill Inc., New York, 1995

In Chapter 17 of the referenced text, the author focuses on typical cycles in production management. Program maintenance is one of the cycles that benefit from a structured and disciplined approach to management. In other words, the tighter things <u>are</u> managed, the tighter they <u>can be</u> managed. This text provides the reader with some thoughts on how it is possible to create management systems that cause repetitive cycles to become increasingly efficient with repetition.

Senge, Peter M.; The Fifth Discipline, The Art & Practice of the Learning Organization; Doubleday Publishing; New York; 1990

In the author's experience, Program Maintenance is often viewed as an activity that can be assigned to individuals who are not as skilled as others. It does not have the visibility or criticality of either routine maintenance or turnaround maintenance. This point of view is costly both in terms of dollars spent and of the equipment integrity that is sacrificed. Using the concepts suggested in the referenced test, the reader can spend less and get more for each dollar spent by applying "learning principles as part of the Program Maintenance Process.

CHAPTER 7
THE PROJECT PROCESS

I'm here to put you back on schedule.
Darth Vader

I want to begin this chapter by saying that there are already more than enough sources of information on project management and execution. There is any number of books on the subject. In addition, many university extension divisions and community colleges offer courses and workshops on project management.

Rather than covering the broad subject of the Project Process, I will confine my comments to a few critical issues that are particularly important Project Man-agement as it relates to Maintenance Excellence. They are:

- Project Definition
- Resource Control
- Accountability Limitations

Project Definition

For scores of years the companies that perform major projects have been known as EPC contractors. This nomenclature tends to reflect the steps of project development and execution they typically perform:

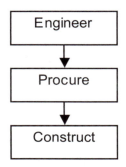

For years these steps were accepted as the way to build plants and other facilities. In more recent years, companies have begun to analyze the results of their capital investment programs more closely, and have found that the results were not what they expected.

- Often significant resources were invested in projects, only to have them wither on the vine for lack of support.
- Occasionally projects were completed only to find they did not meet the perceived intent of all stake holders.
- Projects costs were more than expected because features with little value or ROI were included.
- Significant funds had to be spent to get projects back on track after having strayed.

As a result of these studies, some companies have chosen to re-define their Project Process with more emphasis on the required steps and less emphasis on the typical skills that contractors have to offer.

These steps look more like the following:

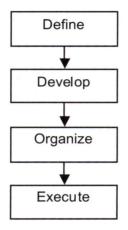

Revisiting the list of problems encountered in previous projects, most of the problems were the result of too little attention being paid during the "Define" step. It is important to describe the desired results in minute detail during this step, when few and (relatively) inexpensive resources are being consumed. It is far better to spend time at this stage in the project development than waste resources later.

Recognizing this requirement, many organizations have introduced a "Stage-Gate" or "Step-Approval" process for defining project requirements. This process incorporates a series of well-defined steps with intervening "gates" or "approvals" to ensure that all the project stake holders remain in agreement with the direction of project development as it takes on increasing levels of detail. This approach has proven to significantly decrease the amount of wasted resources due to re-cycling.

Early steps in the process identify the general results that are desired. These results might include the product slate, capacity, and quality of products. Once there is agreement on basic objectives, additional effort and resources are spent to add detail and understand ultimate project costs, life-cycle costs and anticipated long-term return on investment.

Occasionally at the conclusion of a project, someone will say, "If I knew how much it was going to cost, I never would have started" or "If I knew how long it was going to take, I never would have started". It is important to provide those choices as early as possible.

As each incremental amount of additional information is assembled, it is reported to the project sponsors or steering committee. That group is asked if they continue to support the direction the project is taking. If they do, everything continues down the same path. If not, the project direction is changed or the project is halted.

Although there are occasions where substantial amounts are spent on a project and it is nonetheless cancelled, this iterative approach ensures that it would have been impossible to make the same decision any sooner, or with a smaller investment.

Resource Control

In completing a project, all kinds of resources are involved. Depending on your perspective, and the structure of your organization, the resources are either internal or external to your company. In addition, the resources may be under your administrative control or you may need to coordinate their involvement through "dotted-line" relationships. Personnel may be full-time long-term employees or they may be part time or temporary.

Most projects are done in a finite, limited period of time, so a variety of organizational configurations and reporting relationships are possible.

If you are the Project Manager or are in some way accountable for seeing that the project is completed on budget and on schedule, you need to consider how you will fulfill your accountabilities. There are only three ways in which accountabilities can be fulfilled:

• Control – In this method you have the resources needed to fulfill your accountabilities under your direct administrative control. So you can direct the needed work to be done.
• Influence – If you do not have direct control, you accomplish your accountabilities using your personal skills and charisma. Logic and rational arguments must then be compelling and people must have sufficient resources to perform all requirements including yours. If there are other, more compelling needs, or if there are insufficient resources, no amount or charisma can overcome the limitations.

• Escalate – If you do not have control and you are unable to influence others to cooperate, you must escalate. That means going to a higher authority who can exercise control.

Let's think about using each approach as a Project Manager:

• The effectiveness of control is fairly simple. People either follow instructions or they do not. If they choose not to follow the instructions of their supervisor, they need to be quickly replaced.
• Unless you have exceptional charisma, influence is a pretty hit-or-miss way of completing a project. (Very few Project Managers have any charisma anyway.)
• Escalation is a tool that is effective only if used very sparingly. If you find yourself needing to escalate problems for resolution very frequently, you will quickly be seen as being effete and ineffective.

As a result, the only way a project works well is when the accountable individual has direct administrative control over substantially all the resources needed to complete the project. Beginning a large complex project with a lot of "dotted-line" relationships is a recipe for failure.

Accountability Limitations

The role of a Project manager is really pretty simple. A Project Manager juggles three things:

1. Results or Scope
2. Schedule
3. Budget

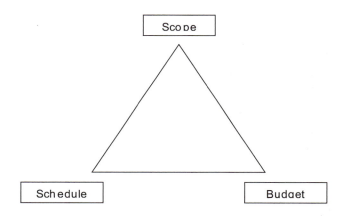

In most plants the accountability assigned to a Project Manager tends to develop over time as the project is developed. As a result, the Project Manager has the ability to influence how the three elements fit together. As a project is developed, the three areas of accountability tend to merge toward a final definition:

- The objective or results are translated into the final work scope.
- The scope is translated into a schedule.
- The scope and schedule are turned into a budget.

Some times management needs a "scope quality" budget early so that advanced capital budgets can be set. The final budget should then be determined after the final scope is determined and the schedule impacts have been factored in. If a shortened schedule requires overtime or weekend work, or if it is necessary to make provision for working in foul weather, the budget will need to be increased.

The point I am making in this discussion is that the three areas of accountability are interdependent. It is unreasonable to rigidly set all three and expect someone to be held accountable for them unless there is fat in the budget or slop in the schedule. It is possible to set the scope and the schedule, but then the budget must have the flexibility to be adjusted to accommodate the other two.

Rather than:

Engineer $\rightarrow$ Procure $\rightarrow$ Construct

The better process for developing a project is:

- Clearly define requirements
- Organize for control.
- Manage accountabilities

Additional Thoughts from References

Lewis, James P.; *Fundamentals of Project Management, Second Edition;* AMACOM, New York; 2001

Like the book that is referenced below, this text provides the reader with a simple and easy read that introduces the critical elements of project management. It seems that, although there are a number of excellent tools like this one, there are still a large number of people being assigned projects who seem unable to organize and execute projects that complete the desired scope on schedule and on budget.

Thomsett,.Michael C. ; *The Little Black Book of Project Management;* AMACOM, New York; 1990

I recall a situation not long ago when I was working with a young engineer on improving his project management skills. It so happened that this discussion occurred in an organization that was quite reactive, and historically did not place a value on being proactive and managing work in a professional manner. After our discussion about improving his project management skills, this gentleman made the comment, "We have tried project management here and it doesn't work". In response, I asked, "Does gravity work here?" Project management skills are kind of like gravity, they work everywhere. The referenced book, while small and simple, is an excellent tool for teaching some of the basic elements of organizing tasks so they can be accomplished in a timely and cost-effective manner.

CHAPTER 8
THE RELIABILITY PROCESS IN
MAINTENANCE EXCELLENCE

Knowing is not enough; we must apply!
EPITICUS

A significant portion of a plant or systems reliability is determined during the initial design and construction. Choices concerning configuration (e.g. redundancy), and robustness, will determine the inherent reliability of the plant or system.

> **Inherent Reliability:**
> **The inherent reliability of a plant, system or device is the maximum achievable reliability based on configuration and component selection. If operated correctly, maintained correctly and inspected on appropriate intervals, it will be possible to attain the full inherent reliability. If poorly operated, poorly maintained or allowed to develop and retain defects, the reliability can be significantly less than the inherent reliability.**

Although the inherent reliability defines the upper limit for performance as initially designed and constructed, work management processes that can be enhanced by Maintenance Excellence will determine:

1. How close to inherent reliability the asset will perform.
2. If the inherent reliability will be increased or decreased as the asset ages and is modified.

Let's discuss these two issues separately.

Achieving Inherent Reliability

The ability to achieve the full inherent reliability of a plant or system depends on restoring the features that determine the inherent reliability whenever maintenance work is done.

For example, when a pump is maintained in a "shortcut" manner, its reliability will not be as good after maintenance as it was before maintenance. In many instances, the reason why equipment is maintained in a "shortcut" manner can be found in the Routine Maintenance Process (RMP) or the Turnaround Process (TAP).

If the RMP in a plant is not running smoothly, backlog will be too high, work will not be done in a timely manner, and people will resort to assigning exaggerated priorities simply to get work done. It is then likely that the plant will begin using shortcut repairs just to get caught up.

On the other hand, if the RMP is working well, repairs will

be performed in a timely and trustworthy manner. Everyone will then support taking the time and spending the resources needed to restore the inherent reliability when equipment is being maintained.

The same is true of the TAP. If the TAP is working poorly, people will need to take shortcuts to achieve schedule and budget. From the standpoint of reliability, shortcuts are indeed shortsighted.

So the Reliability Management Process and the Maintenance Excellence Process go hand-in-hand. If maintenance work management processes are not done in a manner that restores the inherent reliability, the reliability performance will continually degrade. If the Reliability process is not working to provide an acceptable level of reliability, the maintenance processes will end up "chasing-their-tail", dealing with too-frequent and unexpected breakdowns.

In addition to maintaining an asset in a manner that protects the inherent reliability, it is important to maintain it in a manner that achieves the full inherent reliability over the maximum possible life. Think about this concept for a moment. Say a device is capable of 99% reliability. That level of reliability is associated with a specific life-span. The device will not provide the 99% reliability over an infinite life, so it is important to identify end-of-life, and maintain or replace the asset before reliability deteriorates.

An analytical technique called Reliability Centered Maintenance (RCM) is used to identify the optimum maintenance program of predictive and preventive maintenance. RCM-based maintenance will both harvest the available inherent reliability and do so at the minimum lifecycle cost.

The objective of preventive maintenance is to intervene before a failure occurs. The objective of predictive maintenance is to identify the appropriate timing for preventive maintenance. Predictive maintenance allows one to harvest all the usable life without sacrificing reliability.

Later chapters will discuss RCM, predictive maintenance and preventive maintenance in greater detail.

Improving or Reducing Inherent Reliability

Over the life of a plant or system, there are always modifications and "improvements". In some instances, these "improvements' are done in a manner that maintains or improves inherent reliability. In others, the work is done in a manner that degrades the inherent reliability.

If reliability is not considered during the design, and the engineers do not separately and distinctly perform "Design for Reliability", you take what you get. That may be better or worse than the current inherent reliability.

Each and every time a modification is made, there is an opportunity to either improve or reduce the inherent reliability. If, for instance, a change is made that will increase the capacity of a unit but will do so by keeping both the primary and spare feed pump operating continuously. The reliability will be reduced because there is no longer any redundancy.

In another example, if a key component is replaced with one that is less robust; the reliability of the system will suffer.

On the other hand, if a modification is used as an opportunity to address recognized weaknesses, it would be possible to enhance reliability. For instance, if for some time, both the primary and spare feed pump have been used to achieve needed thru-put, a modification program can be used as an opportunity to restore full redundancy.

Another example might involve an electrical distribution that has grown in an uncontrolled manner over time. A modification program might provide an opportunity to balance loads and ensure there is sufficient capacity for unusual but expected fluctuations.

As plants and systems are modified, there is an opportunity to make things better, but there is also the risk of making things worse. The direction will depend on you and the effort you invest into the reliability aspects of the design.

Reliability in the Routine Maintenance Process

Maintenance may be performed in a wide variety of ways. Some of these ways support reliability and others create defects that lead to poor reliability. It is clear that performing a task that intervenes before a failure occurs is less expensive and results in fewer interruptions than waiting for failures to occur before acting. But there is also a variety of ways in which reactive or repair maintenance can be done. Some of them are consistent with improving reliability and others are not.

At one extreme is the old baling wire and chewing gum approach. At the other extreme is the practice of trying to make everything better than new. I support neither extreme.

Baling wire and chewing gum repairs are the result of a "fire-fighting" approach at maintenance. You are never quite sure when the next fire will break out so you are always in a hurry to put out the last one. Rather than restoring inherent reliability by taking the device back to original specifications, this approach simply fixes what is broken up to the point that the device can be placed back in service. The mean time to failure after a repair is frequently a fraction of the MTBF of a new (or properly maintained) device. As more and more short-cut repairs are made, the MTBF will continue to decrease because successively smaller and smaller portions of the equipment will be fit to last the full life.

The other extreme is to try to make everything "better than new" during repairs. I once worked in a refinery where the leader of the rotating equipment discipline viewed every repair as a new re-engineering project. Rather than replacing worn shafts with a new OEM part, he would have them sprayed with a metal coating. Most often this method would result in the bearings needing to be resized and frequently the seals. On all future repairs, the original equipment parts were valueless. Components had to be fabricated from scratch. This approach resulted in longer outage periods and reduced availability. Equipment was out of service longer, so plant reliability and availability suffered.

The best way to perform maintenance is to begin by engineering things correctly, working out any bugs during start-up and early operation, and then maintaining equipment using OEM parts and restoring original tolerance, fits, and clearances. Repair maintenance should restore inherent reliability each and every time without short cuts. Short cuts lead to more short cuts and sooner or later everything in your facility looks like a dog's breakfast.

Reliability in the Turnaround Process

Sooner or later almost every plant or equipment item will need to go through a planned turnaround for major maintenance. Some people call these turnarounds, some call them outages, some call them overhauls, and some call them shutdowns. Whatever you call them, the objective is to restore the equipment to a condition that can provide reliable service until the next planned outage.

In applying reliability management concepts to an outage, the first step is to identify two critical premises. The first premise is the planned duration of the run between this outage and the next one. The second premise is the level of reliability that will be expected between this outage and the next one. These two premises will go a long way toward determining the scope-of-work and the needed condition of the equipment at the conclusion of this outage (the start of the next run). All the items in the plant (or in the equipment being maintained) must be in a condition that will ensure they survive until the next outage.

The next chapter discusses "precision maintenance" or the practice of:

1. Identifying "as-found" conditions at the start of any maintenance activity.
2. Based on the difference between "as-left" conditions (at the end of the previous repair) and "as-found" conditions (at the beginning of this repair), calculating the deterioration rate.
3. Identifying the required "as-left" conditions at the conclusion of the current maintenance, needed to ensure the item will survive the desired run-length.

The same concept as described for "precision maintenance" must be applied to all parts of the plant (or equipment) during an outage to ensure the required reliability for the intended run-length.

Codes that describe requirements for management of uniform corrosion in piping and pressure vessels provide a good example of how precision maintenance concepts can be applied to "force" systems to be reliable for a specific period of time. In those systems, several critical factors are used to characterize the condition and integrity of the system:

MW – Minimum Wall thickness or the thickness of metal needed to safely retain the operating pressure.

CA – Corrosion Allowance or the thickness of metal that can be corroded away before MW is reached.

CR – Corrosion Rate or the rate (in mils per year) at which uniform corrosion is proceeding.

Life – Life is the number or years, the system will survive based on the current corrosion allowance and corrosion rate.

Half Life – Half Life is half of the current remaining life.

Using this system, the metal thickness is measured using ultrasonic or other thickness measuring techniques at regular intervals. The thickness during the prior measurement is analogous to the "as-left" condition. The thickness during the current measurement is analogous to the "as-found" condition. The corrosion rate (or deterioration rate) is calculated as follows:

$$CR = \frac{\text{Prior Thickness (mils) minus Current Thickness (mils)}}{\text{Time between measurements (years)}}$$

The available life is then calculated using the following equation:

$$\text{Life} = \frac{CA \text{ (mils)}}{CR \text{ (mils per year)}}$$

In piping and pressure vessels containing toxic or hazardous materials, it is required that in the next inspection occur at the "half-life". This rule ensures that half of the corrosion allowance is still intact at the next inspection. If some unforeseen event occurs that accelerates the deterioration rate, it is likely that equipment integrity will remain intact and the problem will be discovered before it results in a failure.

This same concept of "managing deterioration" can be applied to other forms of uniform deterioration and wear. The current condition and deterioration rate can be compared to the condition at which a component will no longer be serviceable. If that point occurs after the end of the desired run, repair or refurbishment is not needed. If the minimum serviceable condition will be surpassed some time during the desired run-length, it will be necessary to refurbish the component.

A successful outage (from the standpoint of reliability) is one in which all critical components are inspected, analyzed, and addressed in the manner described above. Equipment and components that can be repaired on-line without causing an outage are the exception. They should be repaired (using precision maintenance methodology) outside the duration of the outage.

Reliability in the Project Process

Expansions and modifications should be treated in the same manner as new equipment and facility designs. Design for Reliability (DFR) should be incorporated within basic design.

I recall one occasion in which a young electrical engineer was taught the basic essence of the Reliability Block Diagram (RBD) analysis as part of a brief reliability training program. At the same time as he was training, a major revision to the electrical distribution system in his plant was being prepared to support a plant expansion. It was not a practice of the engineering contractor to perform DFR or compare the future configuration to the existing configuration using RBD.

Instead, the young engineer performed a RBD analysis and was able to show that the new configuration of the proposed electrical system would result in a substantial loss in reliability from the current configuration. When plant personnel showed corporate management the analysis, they were surprised to see the added risk of failure. Project managers had always described the changes as being "improvements". In this instance, RBD analysis of the revised configuration justified a change in the design and prevented future problems.

Increasing numbers of companies are making some form of Design for Reliability a mandatory part of project development. They are including reliability and availability hurdles with capacity, quality, and efficiency requirements for both green field and modification projects.

Reliability in the Program Process

As a final comment for this chapter, let's discuss the general area of continuation or renewal. Every asset has an annual depreciation rate. Although many assets continue to operate long after depreciation is complete, few operate reliably without reinvestment at a rate close to the depreciation rate.

Let's take two examples that people seldom consider: structures and electronics.

Steel structures are often ignored when re-investment to offset deterioration is considered. While it may not be necessary to re-invest at the tax write-off rate, a significant level of re-investment is needed to ensure structural integrity and appearance.

It is often thought that electronic components become outdated long before they wear out. But that is not always so. Depending on the environment, electronic boards can become overheated or dirty (causing shorts), or be removed and reinstalled numerous times (causing connections to wear out). It is not uncommon for the application to outlive the hardware. In these conditions, on-going reliability depends on replacing elements that might not typically be viewed as wearing components.

By highlighting these two extremes, I hope to point out that you need to consider them and everything in between if you want to maintain inherent reliability over the entire useful life of the asset.

Additional Thoughts from References

Abernethy, Dr. Robert B.; *The New Weibull Handbook – Fifth Edition*; Robert B. Abernethy, North Palm Beach, Florida; 2004

> Increasingly, the business of Maintenance Excellence is becoming more and more scientific. A standard test upon which much of the science of maintenance management is based is the referenced text. This text is viewed as the standard in forecasting failure rates and

forcing the change from reactive maintenance to pro-active maintenance.

Daley, Daniel T.; *The Little Black Book of Reliability Management;* Industrial Press, New York; 2007

The basic premise of the Little Black Book of Maintenance Excellence is to provide the reader with the tools needed to accomplish all the work needed to achieve high reliability and availability. An earlier book by this author was the Little Black Book of Reliability Management, which inspired the current book. It is suggested that the reader refer to this companion book in developing a comprehensive program to address both reliability and maintenance excellence.

Ireson, W. Grant & Coombs, Clyde F. & Moss, Richard Y. ; *Handbook of Reliability Engineering and Management – Second Edition*; McGraw-Hill, New York; 1996

Increasingly educated and intelligent participants in maintenance organizations are asking the question "Why". They want to know why things fail and what can be done to prevent failures and intervene rather than react. The referenced text provides a compre-hensive treatment of the subject of reliability from ini-tial design through inspection, and predictive and pre-ventive maintenance.

CHAPTER 9
RELIABILITY-CENTERED MAINTENANCE (RCM)

There are sadistic scientists who hurry to hunt down errors instead of establishing the truth.

Marie Curie

RCM is one of the forms of Failure Modes and Effects Analysis (FMEA) used to help ensure the reliability and integrity of complex systems by identifying the optimum program of predictive and preventive maintenance. RCM comes in a number of shapes and sizes. It seems that individuals who are advocates of one form of RCM are dead-set opposed to the other forms. Since I have never seen anyone arrested for using the improper form of RCM, I guess we can focus just on improving reliability and leave all the arguing to others.

Depending on how the form of RCM being used is structured, it can do a few things or it can incorporate a number of objectives into one analysis. Individuals who have participated in several of the different forms of FMEA (like Process Hazard Analysis and Risk Based Inspection) will know that there are similarities between these forms of analysis. Similar forms of information must be gathered in preparation for any of these forms of analysis. The content of discussions and workshops, and the participants in those discussions and workshops, are also very similar. The most effective and efficient way to perform these analyses is to design them in a manner that ensures you get the "biggest bang for your buck". My philosophy is to modify the design of the RCM analysis to fulfill all my objectives.

In the following discussion, I will try to describe RCM briefly, but in a general manner. I am sure that this description will not satisfy everyone, but it is a reasonable approach and includes many of the alternatives that are possible. I have included a simplified flow chart describing this process to help the reader follow the sequence of steps.

• The analysis begins by clearly identifying a system or a portion of the plant or asset that will be analyzed. It is important to set clear boundaries because those boundaries are critical in identifying the included functions and in making assumptions.

An example of a boundary issue is where specific isolation valves will be analyzed (e.g. in this system or in an adjacent system). Critical equipment capable of producing failures must clearly be in the system most affected. Another example of a boundary issue is utilities and instrument signals. It is typically assumed that utilities will be supplied and signals will be correct. If there are problems, they will be analyzed in their own systems.

• The next step is to identify the function or functions

performed by the system being analyzed. This is an important step because the function(s) is the characteristic you are trying to preserve. For instance, if the function of a boiler is to produce 100,000 pounds per hour of 100 psi steam, then it is clear that when steam production is halted, the intended function is not being achieved. But how about when the boiler is capable of producing only 90,000 pounds per hour of steam or only 90 psi steam? Is the function being achieved in those instances? It is important to clearly define the "specifications" for the required functions.

Assume also that the boiler makes a certain amount of noise while operating. Is the sound level a critical part of the function? Do you wish to identify pro-active tasks that will preserve the sound level? If so, include this as a part of the definition of the function. If not, don't bother with it.

•   The next step is to identify all the forms of "Functional Failure" (FF). In the example above, if the specification of the function is to produce 100,000 pounds per hour of 100 psi steam at 90 dB or less there are several possible FFs:

1. Boiler is completely shut down.
2. Boiler is producing less than 100,000 pounds per hour of steam.

3. Boiler is producing steam at something less than 100 psi.
4. Boiler is operating at greater than 90 dB.

• The next step is one that depends on choices you have made concerning your form of RCM analysis. The choices involve the economic analysis of the FF. Most analysis conducted for businesses are interested in balancing the cost of prevention with the value of the failure being prevented, so it is important to identify the value of each form of FF. Since the total cost of a specific failure mode varies with the duration of the resulting event, it is required that the cost of each FF be stated in dollars per hour or day.

In the example above, let's assume:

1. When the boiler is down the cost impact is $24,000 per day.
2. When the boiler is producing less than 100,000 pounds per hour (2,400,000 pounds/day), the loss is figured on a sliding scale at $.01 per pound down to 60,000 pounds per hour, below which the boiler cannot operate.
3. When the steam boiler is producing steam at less than 100 psi, let's assume that the receiving system operates at 100 psi, so the steam produced will not make it past the check valve into the system. This condition is tantamount to the boiler being shut down.
4. When the boiler operates at greater than 90 dB for any portion of a day, there is a $10,000 per day fine.

• The next step is to "import" all the equipment and

components that can result in any of the FF(s) when the item fails. Again, there are several choices at this step. Some forms of analysis look at "dynamic" equipment only. This view includes pumps, compressors, instrumentation, control valves ... things that move or regularly change states. This approach would exclude "static" elements like piping and pressure-retaining equipment. The choice of what should be included should be based on which components regularly contribute to the "unreliability".

Another choice has to do with the kind of analysis you are performing. If you are performing a "critical" analysis, you will import only the items that can cause an FF. An alternative is to import all equipment, including those items where a failure will not result in an FF. The logic of analyzing "non-critical" equipment is that there is a value in balancing pro-active tasks with reactive tasks for items where the cost of failure is high. In other words, there are instances where an ounce of prevention is worth a pound of cure. (If the system or software being used is set up to compare the cost of PM to the total cost of failure, you can perform a "non-critical" analysis at the same time you perform the "critical analysis.)

• The next step is to identify the "failure modes" for each item you have decided to include in the analysis. This point provides another choice. "Classical" RCM looks at all possible failure modes. "Streamlined" RCM looks only at those failure modes that have happened in the past and are likely to happen again in the future. (These are called Dominant Failure Modes

(DFM)). If the RCM analysis is being done to support safety through absolutely reliable operation (as with an aircraft, or a nuclear power plant), the former choice might be best. If the objective is to enhance reliability by developing a cost-effective maintenance program that focuses resources on areas of greatest risk to reliability, the latter approach is the most appropriate.

• The next step is to go through each item and characterize the current situation concerning the failure mode(s) and effect(s). This step will completely describe the current economics.

1. What is the DFM?
2. What FF does it cause?
3. What is the Mean Time Between Failure (MTBF)?
4. What is the annual likelihood of an event?
5. How long will the FF last when this failure mode occurs?
6. What is the cost of repairs associated with this failure mode?

• Now you can calculate the value of the annual current risk. Again, here is a point at which choices are possible. Some systems tend to simplify the risk calculations by assuming that the annual likelihood of failure is one divided by the MTBF. This approach assumes that each year has a nearly equal likelihood of producing a failure. Other approaches use Weibull analysis to calculate the likelihood. Other systems use the statistical likelihood that results from modeling. At the end of the day, the objective is to quantify the reduction in risk associated with applying some form of prevention. For the sake of clarity, I will use the simplified approach in this discussion.

The calculation of value of current annual risk is accomplished as follows:

Risk = Impact x Likelihood
Impact = (Hourly or daily value of FF x Days or
        hours out of service)
    + Cost of Repairs
Likelihood = 1 / MMBF

Extending the example from above, assume that the boiler system has only one boiler feed water (BFW) pump and:
• It has a history of failing every seven years.
• When it fails, it requires seven days to repair.
• When it fails, the boiler is completely down.
• When it fails without warning, it costs $25,000 to repair.

The value of the annual risk is:

Impact   = ($24,000/day x 7 days) + $25,000
              = $193,000
Likelihood = 1 per 7 years = 0.1428 per year
Annual Risk = $193,000 x 0.1428
              = $25,571.

• The next step is to identify the possible forms of prevention and quantify their impact.

One possibility is to implement some form of predictive maintenance. Predictive maintenance could take the form of vibration analysis, oil sampling, or any of a number of non-invasive tasks. A predictive task may not prevent an outage, but it might provide enough warning so that the owner could be prepared. The warning might reduce the duration of the outage or reduce the cost of the event by avoiding some of the damage resulting from a catastrophic failure. Another possibility is that predictive maintenance might both limit the cost and the duration of the outage by providing for a limited repair (say replacing a bearing rather than overhauling a wreck).

Another possibility is to implement some form of preventive maintenance. If the failure mode is wear out and it can be reliably predicted, it may be possible to intervene and eliminate an unplanned event. For instance if the failure occurs at the end of the seven-year life (rather than randomly throughout the seven years), it would be possible to pro-actively change out the pump at the six-year point or during the last planned outage before the predicted failure. This approach would significantly reduce the risk of unplanned failure.

Another possibility is to implement some form of physical change to the system, like installing a spare BFW pump, or replacing the current pump with one that is more reliable. Where risk is high and the need for reliability is great, redundant equipment is justified. With installed spares, simplified pro-active maintenance tasks like operator observations may be sufficient to

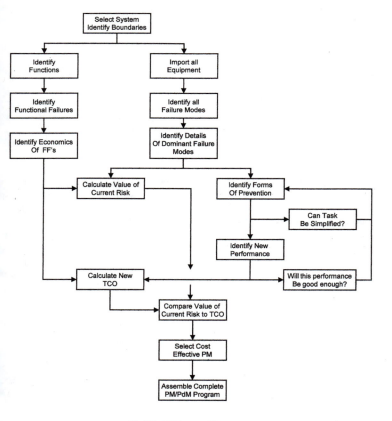

RCM Flow Chart

switch pumps in a timely manner and completely eliminate any significant risk of an outage caused by an
unexpected failure.

RCM Flow Chart

In each of the three examples cited above, it would be
necessary to calculate the annual cost of prevention
and add that to the reduced value of annual risk
resulting from the modification, to understand the new
total cost of ownership with prevention.

As a worked example, let's assume that the recommended solution involves the performance of some
form of preventive maintenance. Assume that the PM
being recommended is to be performed weekly and
will cost $250 per instance.

The total cost of the recommended prevention would
be:

$$PM = \$250 \times 52 = \$13,000$$

Now let's assume that we are confident, based on earlier experience, that this form of PM will extend the life
to ten years. Therefore the new MTBF is 10 and the
new likelihood of failure is 1 / 10 or 0.10.

The total cost of ownership (TCO) with the new preventive maintenance is:

$$
\begin{aligned}
TCO \quad &= \text{New risk} + \text{Cost of PM} \\
&= (\$193,00 \times .1) + \$13,000 \\
&= \$32,300
\end{aligned}
$$

In this example, the TCO with PM is more costly than that without PM, so it would **not** be cost effective to apply the recommended PM.

This kind of result is frequently encountered. In the example, one might:

- Look for other forms of PM that are less costly.
- Consider performing the task less frequently.
- Investigate whether other tasks are more effective at extending the life and reducing the likelihood of failure.

When considering the alternative, of installing a spare pump, another way to compare the cost of installing the spare pump with the value resulting from improved reliability would be to compare the Net Present Value of all future risks that are avoided, with the current cost of installing the spare pump.

Each form of prevention may produce a different form or reliability improvement. Some forms of prevention may reduce the likelihood of failure. Some may reduce the impact of the failure by reducing the duration of the outage or the extent of the FF. Still others might reduce the extent of the damage (to the pump) and the resulting cost of repair.

The objective of the analysis is to:

- Understand the current relationship between failure modes and effects.
- Identify some form of prevention that attacks

the failure mode and/or reduces the effect.

• The next step in the RCM analysis is to continue this analysis through all the items that have been chosen for analysis and imported.

• Two final steps are needed to produce results that are both practical and pragmatic. The first final step is to compare all the new recommendations for the pro-active maintenance program with the current program. It is frequently best to roll the new program out over a period of time so that personnel have time to absorb the changes.

• The second of the final two steps is to overlay all pro-active maintenance programs onto a single spreadsheet. This procedure will frequently make programs more efficient by moving some tasks a little earlier and other tasks a little later, so that crews can address more things at once.

There is an old joke by comedian George Burns in which he said, "You can tell you are getting old by when you bend over to tie your shoe, you think about what other things you can do while you are down there." Efficiently-organized maintenance takes advantage of the wisdom of this joke.

In organizing a RCM program, there is a variety of other choices that can be made in terms of functionality and resulting recommendations.

One of these choices is the inclusion of an additional step

at the conclusion of the analysis of each item. That step is simply asking the question "Is this good enough?" It is possible that, despite the amount of improvement that will result from your recommendations, the performance will still not be good enough. If the answer is that the performance will still not be adequate, it might be necessary to perform Root Cause Analysis or some other more-directed form of engineering analysis, to produce the required performance.

The second choice has to do with who does the work being recommended, and how the work will be done. Many pro-active maintenance tasks can be performed by journeyman craftsmen, or they can be simplified and performed by the operator. An example is vibration analysis. Ask yourself, "Can my objective be equally well met by an operator simply laying his hand on the bearing housing each shift to see if the vibration level has increased?" This approach may eliminate the need for an expensive vibration technician. It will also cause the operator to become more intimately familiar with his equipment and allow the task to be done once or more every shift rather than on some less-frequent basis.

If RCM is used in this manner, it provides an excellent tool for populating the operating rounds in plants using Operator Driven Reliability (ODR) or Total Productive Maintenance (TPM).

In conclusion, RCM is most often viewed as a tool to identify an optimized program of predictive and preventive maintenance. The objective is to achieve the lowest overall lifecycle cost, including the cost of asset loss resulting from failure-caused outages. RCM is designed to exploit the maximum inherent reliability of the current system

If you are smart, like George Burns, there are some other things you can do while conducting an RCM analysis:

1. Further improve inherent reliability by identifying and addressing current performance limiters that do not meet expectations.
2. Optimize the use of all the resources in your organization by identifying simplified tasks that will enhance the reliability performance of your equipment.

Additional Thoughts from References

Smith, Anthony M., Reliability Centered Maintenance, McGraw-Hill Inc., New York, 1993

> The referenced text provides one of the earliest treatments of RCM analysis as a separate and distinct analysis. It is a useful baseline in understanding the starting point for this useful form of analysis.

Daley, Daniel T.; The Little Black Book of Reliability Management; Industrial Press, New York; 2007

> Over time, interest and support for engineering analysis using one or another form of Failure Modes and Effects Analysis (FMEA) has grown. At the same time, resource managers have asked for more efficient

ways to "kill two or more birds with one stone". The above reference provides the reader with thoughts and concepts that will be useful in achieving improved resource efficiency while not sacrificing the effectiveness of the analysis. RCM, Risk Based Inspection, and Process Hazard Analysis, are all FMEAs using much the same information and involving many of the same people. If these disciplines are carefully integrated, it will be possible to derive many of benefits viewed as being discretionary while fulfilling mandatory requirements.

CHAPTER 10
PREDICTIVE MAINTENANCE

What we see depends mainly on what we look for.
John Lubbock

One of my favorite stories is the story of little Johnny, the optimist.

Little Johnny was a boy about eight years old who was growing up in a poor family. Despite the hard conditions, little Johnny remained an optimist. Whenever his parents would see little Johnny in his torn and tattered hand-me down clothes, they could be certain he would have a smile on his face. As time passed, conditions continued to be bad. With never a reason for a glint of hope, little Johnny remained positive. Finally, little Johnny's birthday arrived, and Johnny told his parents that he wanted above all, a pony for his birthday. As it turned out, his father was out of work, the rent was long past due, and the cupboard was bare. Had there been any money there were many priorities ahead of a birthday gift for little Johnny but, alas, there was no money. To add to the bleakness of the day, a dump truck hauling a load of horse manure was misdirected and somehow managed to dump a huge pile of horse dung on the driveway leading to Johnny's house. The smell was overwhelming and it was unlikely that the mess would soon be removed. Rather than grimacing, when Johnny caught wind of the delivery his round face broke out in a big smile and he immediately went out to the manure pile and began digging through it with his hands. Wondering what he was thinking, his mother went out to find little Johnny arms deep in the foul wet manure. Dismayed his mother asked Johnny what he was doing. Through a wide grin beaming from that freckled face covered with manure, Johnny responded, "With this much horse poop, there's got to be a pony in there somewhere."

I began this chapter with this story because it is the best description of optimism that I know, and predictive maintenance is maintenance intended for optimists. Predictive Maintenance is based on the belief that it is possible to find defects and intervene before a failure or (in some events), significant deterioration, can occur.

This chapter will discuss "predictive maintenance" and the next chapter will discuss "preventive maintenance". Some people tend to mix the two, but I like to think of them as being separate and distinct.

Both Predictive and Preventive maintenance tasks are Pro-active. The reason is that they are done without being stimulated by a failure. These tasks occur before a failure, and prevent it.

Predictive maintenance is typically non-invasive and consists of searching for conditions that can cause deterioration and lead to failure. On the other hand, Preventive Maintenance is frequently invasive and is intended to deal with a condition that is already known to exist.

For instance if I check a fluid level, that is a predictive step. If I know that the fluid is consumed at a known rate and I have a task to replenish the fluid, that is a preventive task.

As a part of describing "predictive maintenance", it is helpful to understand the typical "Path to Failure". The chart below shows the steps of that path.

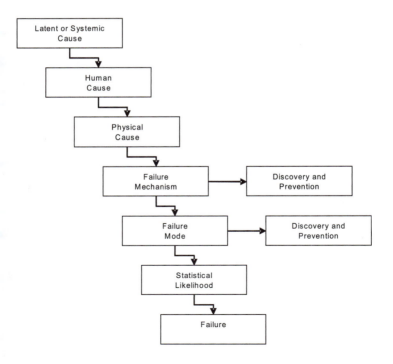

The path begins with a "latent or systemic cause" or a situation that exists within your organization, processes, or procedures, that allows one of your employees to fail.

The next step is the "human cause, which is the instance in which one of your employees steps into the trap created by the latent or systemic cause and either performs an act or omits an act that creates a physical cause.

The "physical cause" comes next, and is a specific condition resulting from the action or omission mentioned above, that creates a condition where one of the Failure Mechanisms can begin its work.

The Failure Mechanism is one of the forms of deterioration that ultimately can result in a defect. During the time that a failure mechanism is at work, it is possible to recognize its presence and intervene.

After the failure mechanism has been at work for a sufficient period of time, a defect will form. The defect is the condition that opens the door for a failure to occur. Again, as with the Failure Mechanism, it is possible to identify the presence of a defect and intervene before a failure takes place.

Once a defect exists, nature starts rolling the dice. In some conditions, the odds of failure are "long". In other words, there is still a low likelihood that a failure will occur. In other situations, the odds are "short" or even one-to-one, meaning that as soon as the defect exists, a failure will occur.

The failure is best described as the loss of a critical function. It also can be described by identifying the function that is no longer being provided and the behavior that is being exhibited.

An example of a Path to Failure is as follows:
- A plant has no procedure for communicating work status from the end of one shift to the beginning of the next shift. (Latent cause).
- Joe installs a piping system that requires a support to prevent it from vibrating. At the end of his shift, Joe has completed the piping but not the support. John starts the beginning of the next shift but does not recognize that the support is missing so he signs the job off as complete. (Human cause).
- Without the support, the piping system vibrates. (Physical cause).
- The level of vibration is beyond the fatigue limit of the piping elements. In a specific number of fatigue cycles, the piping system will form a crack. (Failure Mechanism).
- After a few weeks, a small cracks forms in the pipe. (Failure Mode).
- After a few more days, the normal maximum operating pressure is reached and a major leak occurs. (End of the statistical likelihood).
- As a result of the leak, the affected system shuts down, and the critical function is lost. (Failure).

The value of understanding the Path to Failure is knowing that both the Failure mechanism and the Defect can be discovered before failure, and that the failure can be prevented. Wise people also learn from failures, and they identify the three levels of cause in time to take corrective action.

In order to create Predictive Maintenance tasks, you need to understand the failure mechanisms that "are" at work and those that "can be" at work. That is an important point to emphasize. Many people simply copy the PM tasks recommended by the manufacturer, and then perform them by rote without really understanding why they are doing them.

Predictive Maintenance tasks are intended to:
1. Evaluate failure mechanisms that are known to be at work.
2. Identify failure mechanisms that can be at work.

Let's describe both of these instances with examples.

The lives of many components and subsystems can best be described using a "bathtub curve". The "bathtub" curve is a graph of the statistical likely of failure over the life of the component. It consists of three parts.

The first part of the curve is an exponentially decreasing line describing "infant mortality"or "infantile failures". As the name implies this curve represents the likelihood of failures caused by some form of defect that is associated with manufacture. As the component "survives" early life, the increased likelihood of failure during this period goes away. This kind of failure is particularly common in electronic components and systems made up of a number of electronic components. As a result, many electronic components and systems are exposed to "burn in" to ensure

the products delivered to customers will have already survived the "infantile failure" period.

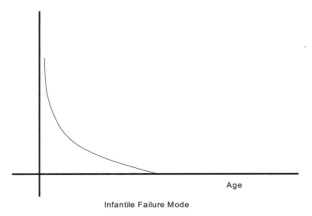

Infantile Failure Mode

The second part of the curve is a long period of fairly
small likelihood of failure. Once through the infantile period, the likelihood of failure for proven components is typically small, but not zero. Throughout the life, some small

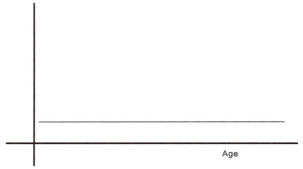

Random Failure Mode

numbers of random failures continue to occur during each measurement period.

The third part of the curve is an exponentially increasing likelihood of failure that is associated with "end-of-life". This upward trend is probably the most critical part of the bathtub curve, and also the least well understood.

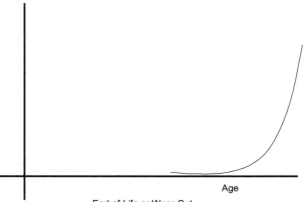

Age

End-of-Life or Wear-Out

A variety of failure mechanisms may be at work leading to an increased likelihood of failure at the end-of-life. An example is fatigue. Many mechanical components operate reliably for long periods, during which fatigue cycles are mounting. Finally, at some point, based on the statistic of a normal distribution, the component reaches the end of its fatigue life and failure begins to occur.

Adding all three components together results in a composite curve that represents the overall life of a component or system. This curve takes the shape of a "bathtub" thus the name "bathtub curve".

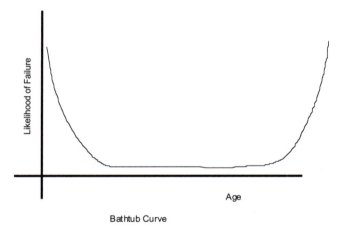

Bathtub Curve

On occasion, when teaching people about this concept, students have extended the metaphor by saying that their plants were no longer operating in the "bathtub". Instead they were operating out on the "towel rack". This comment was meant to describe a condition where all the practically useful life was gone and the plant was operating in a region where the likelihood of failure was high.

Building on the analogy, let's discuss the value of understanding the "bathtub curve". The greatest value comes with finding the "drain". In a typical bathtub, the "drain" is located at the transition between the period of low random failure and the beginning of end-of-life failures.

While we may "think" we know the location of this point

we often do not. Finding the "drain" is the real value of predictive maintenance because it pertains to failure mechanisms that are known to be at work.

In explaining this situation, I like to use the analogy of the "bathtub curve" for physical systems with the "bathtub curve" for human life. As with the likelihood of fatality for a human, there is an increased likelihood as an infant, a long and relatively low likelihood between infancy and old age, and an increasing likelihood at old age.

I also like to use my mother as an example of the problem with using the bathtub curve to identify preventive maintenance rather than predictive maintenance at the perceived onset of old-age. As I am writing this chapter, my mother is more than eighty-eight and a half years old. Also, as of this writing, the expected life span of humans in the United States is seventy-nine and a half years. In other words, my mother has lived more than nine years past the statistical average.

In the maintenance business, it is not uncommon to think of replacing components at the end of their statistical life. If you were to ask my mother if she is ready to be "replaced" I believe she would object, believing that she is still able to continue performing her intended function for more time.

In many instances we don't really know where the "drain" is located.

Take the example of an anti-friction bearing in a pump. It is possible to look in a catalog and find the B-10 life for the bearing. Some folks might interpret the B-10 as a good time to plan a preventive task to exchange the bearing.

On the other hand let's think for a moment how long the bearing is likely to survive. The B-10 life is the life at which 10% of the bearing population will have failed at rated conditions (load, speed, etc).

Now let's make a few reasonable assumptions.

1. The designer of the pump included a 15% safety factor when specifying the bearing so that the typical maximum load will be 15% less than the design load.
2. The individual who selected the parts from the supplier's catalog found that the required bearing was between two other bearings listed in the catalog. He selected the next larger bearing, so his choice resulted in more excess capacity.
3. Once fabricated and installed, the owner did a better job of installing the pump than the designer assumed, so loading due to misalignment was less.
4. The owner did a better job of maintaining the pump than the designer assumed so that deterioration due to mis-operation or poor maintenance was less.
5. The actual pumping application operated at maximum capacity for only a small part of the time. So bearing loading and operating speed were far less than expected.

Combining the effects of all these assumptions could result in an actual life that is several times as long as the advertised B-10 life (or the change-out period listed in OEM Maintenance manuals).

As a result, the actual bathtub curve looks as follows:

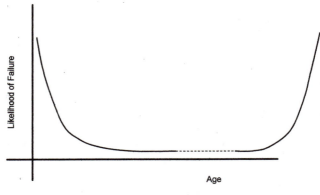

Bathtub Curve – Unknown End-of-Life

In this diagram, the dashed line represents the period in question. It represents the time between when the end-of-life condition might be beginning and when it is actually beginning.

Rather than creating a preventive task at the "drain" point, it is better to create a predictive task at this point. The predictive task needs to be able to identify signals that are characteristic of end-of-life conditions. For instance, vibration might increase, noise might increase, operating temperature might increase, fatigue cracks might begin to appear, etc.

If you are dealing with a large population of components (like a fleet), and predictive maintenance has confirmed that end-of-life has been entered, it is the right time to introduce a preventive task, but not before.

As mentioned earlier, the second reason for performing predictive maintenance is to identify failure mechanisms that can be at work (but are not known to be at work.) Once again, referring back to the "path of failure", defects result from instances where a failure mechanism is allowed to work until the deterioration causes a defect to exist. Once this defect exists, the failure becomes a simple matter of statistics. Whenever things are right (or wrong) the failure will occur.

So, let's discuss predictive maintenance intended to find unknown failure mechanism. For mechanical components, the failure mechanisms are:

- Corrosion
- Erosion
- Fatigue
- Overload

A common unexpected failure mechanism is corrosion. We anticipate and manage many forms of corrosion, so why are there so many situations in which it is unanticipated?

There are a variety of ways in which corrosion can occur, and avoiding them requires vigilance that occasionally is missed.

Let's use a real life example. Batteries are perfect systems to produce corrosion. As a matter of fact, liquid cell battery designs are based on the elements of corrosion:

- Cathode
- Anode
- Electrolyte

As a result, most people understand that batteries are "corrosion machines", and these are specific maintenance tasks involving batteries.

What about the components surrounding the batteries? What if the battery is located under a metal access panel that is also part of a walkway (as they are on some locomotives)? The access panel is likely to flex when it supports the weight of a person, and flexing is likely to result in fine cracks in the protective coating. These batteries see hard service in a variety of weather extremes and they frequently "off-gas", resulting in surrounding components being exposed to sulfuric acid gases. These gases condense back into liquid acids, and surrounding components thus become "corrosion machines".

While the process is not specifically anticipated, it is one that should be observed as part of predictive maintenance.

If individuals who perform other forms of maintenance are made aware of failure mechanisms and forms of deterioration, they can perform predictive maintenance while performing other tasks.

Thus, predictive maintenance can help to identify failure mechanisms that have not been previously identified. Predictive maintenance should include general inspections that produce an awareness of overall condition.

Part of TPM or ODR tasks and part of every PM, PDM and RM task should be overall general inspection that will produce awareness of the other things that are going on in your system.

Additional Thoughts from References

Ireson, W. Grant & Coombs, Clyde F& Moss, Richard Y. ; *Handbook of Reliability Engineering and Management – Second Edition;* McGraw-Hill, New York; 1996

> Predictive maintenance depends to a large degree on some general knowledge of when a device is expected to fail. Individuals who were involved in early forms of RCM will recall that the methods had limited usefulness because they prescribed more tasks than could be reasonably expected to be accomplished. Many of these were predictive tasks that were designed to look for indications of end-of-life when there was little or no knowledge of what was reasonable to expect. As a result, people began looking for end-of-life signs almost as soon as the device was placed into service. The referenced book will be useful to the reader who wants to learn more about the myriad techniques that are available to provide a reasonable estimate of life span, and therefore the proper time to begin to apply predictive maintenance.

O'Connor, Patrick D. T. ; *Practical Reliability Engineering – Fourth Edition;* John Wiley & Sons, LTD; West Sussex, England; 2002

This text is much like the one above in terms of coverage, but the background of the author is different, so the point of view is also somewhat different.

The author of this book has a long and successful career in quality management and tends to view issues from that perspective. Both perspectives are equally valid and useful to the maintenance and reliability professional.

CHAPTER 11
PREVENTIVE MAINTENANCE

I long to accomplish great and noble tasks, but it is my chief duty to accomplish humble tasks as though they were great and noble. The world is moved along, not only by the mighty shoves of its heroes, but also by the aggregate of the tiny pushes of each honest worker.

Helen Keller

The previous chapter provided a brief introduction to Preventive Maintenance. Generally speaking, preventive maintenance is also pro-active but differs from predictive maintenance by the fact it typically includes an invasive task.

For instance, I might use vibration analysis as a predictive task up to the point that I am convinced a bearing is starting to fail. At that point, I will pro-actively change the bearing before a failure can occur. If I was involved with the maintenance of a large fleet of equipment using the same bearing in the same application after a number of similar experiences, I would be satisfied that the component has a specific life. (Here one might use Weibull analysis to determine the usable life.) Once the usable

life has been determined it would become possible to perform preventive maintenance at the appropriate time. By
doing so, I would prevent the majority of failure and at the
same time, harvest most of the usable life.

In that last sentence, I introduced two limitations. I said I
would prevent "most" of the failures and I would harvest
"most" of the life. In attempting to harvest most of the
usable life, I must be willing to accept a small number of
failures. As with anything that fails based on a statistical
distribution, there are always a number of "outliers" that
fail earlier than the general population. If I wanted to
avoid failures associated with these early failures, I would
have to sacrifice a portion of the useful life available from
the majority of the population.

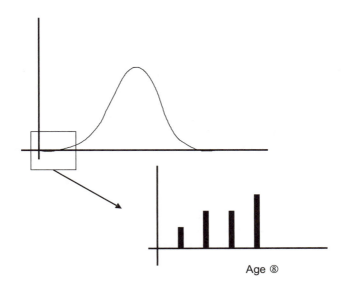

Age ⑧

The opposite is also true, if I wanted to harvest "all" the available life. I would have to experience a significant number of failures before replacement. For instance, if I were to harvest the mean life of a population before beginning to pro-actively replace a component, I would experience a number of failures equal to half the population. Most people would view that as being unscientific and unacceptable. That would be like closing the barn door after the horse has run away.

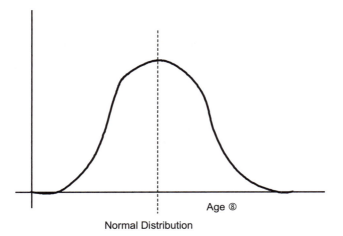

Age ⑧

Normal Distribution

Although much of preventive maintenance is based on the philosophy described above (identifying the end of usable life), there is more to it than that. Few components are efficiently maintained on an individual basis. The secret of effective and efficient preventive maintenance is to determine what other maintenance should be accomplished at the same time as the element that has reached the end of its life. As mentioned earlier, preventive maintenance is typically an invasive activity. Once you have gone to the trouble to take an equipment item apart to replace a component, you should consider:

1. What else should be maintained while the equipment is apart?
2. What do I need to do to reset the clock so that the entire equipment experiences the desired MTBF after re-assembly?
3. What do I need to do to ensure I am not introducing more defects than I am removing?
4. What do I need to do to ensure that this equipment does not experience infantile failure after completion of maintenance?

Preventive Maintenance is a tool that is useful in "forcing" the transition from being reactive to being pro-active. In addition, it can be a tool that is useful in forcing your equipment to survive the targeted MTBF you desire. But it takes planning and some degree of patience.

It is not uncommon for people to adhere to the philosophy "Fix what's broken". That attitude results in addressing only the specific item that has failed or, with preventive maintenance, only the component that is close to failure.

To adopt the philosophy, "Maximize the MTBF", you will need to do several things when you do choose to perform preventive maintenance:

1. You will need to restore the usable life of all worn components, not just the one that is nearing end-

of-life.
2. You will need to understand which component(s) are determining the life of the equipment and the order of failure. To increase MTBF you will need to make the component(s) with the shortest life, more robust.

The order in which components fail, and the length of component lives, can have a variety of patterns. It would be nice if there was a single component with a short life and all the other components had long lives. The following chart describes the life spans of parts that determine the overall life of Equipment Item A. This equipment item has one item with a short life and all other parts have longer lives.

Equipment Item A

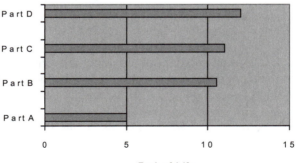

In this example, by investing the resources needed to make Part A more robust, the life of the entire equipment item (consisting of Parts A, B, C, and D) could be significantly extended.

In the example described by the graph shown on the last page, Part A would fail twice for every failure of Parts B, C, and D. So, every other normal maintenance, only Part A would be changed. If it were possible to select a different Part A, or somehow make Part A as robust as Parts B, C, and D, it would be possible to double the MTBF of the overall equipment item.

Equipment Item B

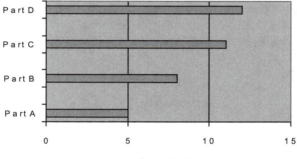

End of Life

Now let's look at another pattern of component life within an equipment item. Once again, the equipment item is made up of wearing Parts A, B, C, and D.

Once again, component A has a useful life that is roughly half that of components C and D. But in this example, component B has a life longer than A but less than C and D. If the maintenance cycle is determined by the life of component A, both components A and B would need to be maintained (because if left un-maintained, B will not last till the end of the second life of component A.) Also, to double the usable life of the equipment item, both components A and B will need to be made more robust.

You might be saying to yourself, "This stuff isn't rocket science. Why is he explaining it in such mind-numbing detail?" The reason is experience. I have experienced numerous times that significant amounts of resources are invested in the one component that fails first, only to have another component fail shortly afterward.

The real difficulty of preventive maintenance is with the people who have a hard time believing the data. They see bearings removed that "appear" to be in good shape and they criticize the program for wasting money. They see situations when maintenance is asked to remove "perfectly good" equipment from service and they criticize the program for wasting money and usable capacity.

In this situation, there is no winning. You are criticized for performing the preventive maintenance and, if you give in to their pressure and do not perform the preventive maintenance, you are criticized when something fails.

The only thing that stops the criticism is comparison of long term trends. Showing that overall reliability, overall availability, overall costs, and overall profitability improve with pro-active maintenance ensures the support of decision makers.

Additional Thoughts from References

Ireson, W. Grant & Coombs, Clyde F. & Moss, Richard Y. ; Handbook of Reliability Engineering and Management – Second Edition; McGraw-Hill, New York; 1996

Many of the same comments that were provided at the end of the last chapter are equally applicable here if not more so. Practices that introduce preventive maintenance earlier than needed will add cost without attendant value.

O'Connor, Patrick D. T. ; Practical Reliability Engineering – Fourth Edition; John Wiley & Sons, LTD; West Sussex, England; 2002

Ditto the comments from above.

Wireman, Terry; World Class Maintenance Management; Industrial Press, New York; 1990

In the referenced text, the author spends a great deal of time focusing on both predictive and preventive maintenance. Maintenance and reliability experts agree that effective and efficient maintenance depends on good reliability. In turn, reliability depends on being pro-active rather than reactive.

CHAPTER 12
PRECISION MAINTENANCE

Arriving at one point may be the starting point for another.

John Dewey

To begin this chapter, think about the engine in your car. Think about the pistons, the cylinders, the valves, the camshaft, the crankshaft, and the bearings. Think about all these things as you are traveling down the highway at 75 miles per hour at night, in a blizzard, with your family in the car. Think about how precisely things need to fit together and how much you depend on the reliability of your engine. Think about the attention and care that was given when the engine was originally assembled.

Now assume that you own a car that was used when you purchased it. Further assume that the engine had been rebuilt sometime while the prior owner had it. Now think about the attention and care that the engine was given when it was being rebuilt.

Compare the mental image you had of the first assembly of a new engine with the image you have of the engine being rebuilt. What were the differences, or do you believe that both procedures were substantially the same?

- Were the bearings replaced?
- How were they fitted to the shaft?
- Were the pistons replaced?
- How were the replacement pistons chosen?
- Was any effort made to ensure that the pistons were balanced?
- How much wear was present on the surfaces of the • camshaft?
- Were the valves worn?
- What was the condition of the valve springs?

For that matter, what did the person performing the work look like?

Did the mechanic assembling precision components have clean hands?
Is the shop clean?

There are a million questions one can ask and the answer is simply, a rebuild is unlike the initial assembly. And you only have the right to expect what has been specified.

Increasing numbers of companies are discovering the value of a process called precision maintenance.

Precision maintenance is a process used in rebuilding or overhauling equipment that incorporates the following elements:

1. The dimensions of each critical tolerance, fit-up, and clearance, are identified by the manufacturer. The manufacturer identifies the normal conditions and the minimum standards needed to ensure advertised performance can be achieved.
2. During assembly, the "as-left" conditions are recorded as needed to provide a basis for calculating the deterioration rate in the future.
3. During disassembly, "as-found" conditions are recorded as needed to compare to the previous "as-left" conditions to determine amount of wear, and wear rate.
4. A "deterioration rate" (DR) is calculated for each critical wearing component using the equation:

$$DR = \frac{\text{"As-found" - "As-left"}}{\text{Time in Service}}$$

5. In preparing for assembly, the expected "end-of-run" (EOR) conditions are calculated using the following equation:

$$EOR = \text{Current condition} - (DR \times \text{Targeted run length})$$

6. If the end-of-run conditions do not meet the minimum standards set by the manufacturer, the affected wearing component is replaced or reconditioned.
7. In addition, all replacement parts are inspected for condition. For example, if pistons are replaced,

they are checked for balance. If pistons are beyond an established tolerance, another group is selected from a much larger population until matching pistons are found.

Any company that has been using precision maintenance for any significant period of time has a number of horror stories concerning the condition of so-called "new" components. In one instance, where an anti-friction bearing was being replaced because of "rough" operation, ten "new" bearings were withdrawn from the warehouse and inspected. All except one operated as roughly as the bearing that was being replaced.

In another instance, a pump supplier changed sources for case castings. It turned out that a third-world supplier provided cases with casting defects that nearly penetrated the wall of the pump case. In yet another instance, improper metallurgy was used for parts and fasteners.

And on, and on. The bottom line is that although many manufacturers have adequate quality control and quality assurance procedures, some do not. When it comes to overhauls and rebuilds, you only get what you specify, and then only when you randomly audit to ensure specifications are being followed.

Additional Thoughts from References

Latino, Robert J. & Latino, Kenneth C. ; *Root Cause Analysis – Improving Performance for Bottom Line Results*; CRC Press, New York; 1999

Although you will not find a direct reference to Precision Maintenance in the reference cited above, I would like to give credit for coining the term precision maintenance to the authors of that book. In addition to providing one of the first and best-organized techniques for approaching root cause analysis, the Latino family has provided the organized thinking behind a number of other improvements in reliability analysis.

CHAPTER 13
THE OPERATOR'S ROLE IN MAINTENANCE EXCELLENCE

The world is a dangerous place, not because of those who do evil, but because of those who look on and do nothing.

Albert Einstein

In the past twenty years or so there have been several movements to increase the operator's role in maintaining the equipment they operate. One such movement was called "operator maintenance" and was an attempt to use operators' "free time" to perform some maintenance tasks. I recall instances where operators were asked to demolish dormant piping, maintain steam traps, and turn blinds.

I place the term "free time" in quotes because it is not uncommon to see operators sitting around control rooms, apparently with nothing better to do. In reality, "free time" is more a matter of poor supervision that it is a lack of things needing to be done. It is important to view operators' time as being quite valuable. The alternative to a task that involves the operator in maintenance is not sitting around the control room. The alternative is some valuable operating task. If an operator is allowed to sit doing nothing, he will do so independently, whether additional tasks are identified or not.

Another approach is called Total Productive Maintenance or TPM. Much of the original literature concerning TPM came from experience applying that approach in Japan. Many of the concepts were good, but it seemed that Americans tended to resist the notion that another country could create an approach that was superior to something that was created in America.

Still another approach is called Operator Driven Reliability or ODR. While ODR has more of a distinctly American flavor, it aims at achieving many of the same objectives as TPM.

I have had the opportunity to observe and participate in all three of these approaches and several examples of each version. One point is certain, even with the highly-ritualistic TPM; no two plants do things in the same way. After all is said and done, the main concern should be to find an approach that works for the special needs of your own plant or shop.

Rather than using any of the three terms described above, I would prefer to avoid the disagreement that may cause. Instead, I will describe an approach I will call ORM or Operator Role in Maintenance. ORM will incorporate some but not all the elements of the three systems described above.

So what is ORM? My guess is that you already know the

answer to that question.. Let's think about ORM in terms of your own car.

What do you want from your car?

- You want it to run all the time when you need it.
- You want it to perform all its functions properly.
- You don't want to replace it too frequently or spend needless money on repairs.

As an owner, there are certain things you are willing to do to achieve that level of performance:

- You will operate it in a manner that does not cause undue wear.
- You will keep it clean. (This means clean enough so that no signs of damage or deterioration become apparent.)
- You will monitor gauges and fluid levels.
- You will either change oil and check tire pressure or pay someone else to do those things regularly.
- You will perform some simple tasks like changing the air filter, fuses, and light bulbs.
- You will keep track of unusual sounds or operations and you will quickly take the car to a shop when you believe an issue is beyond your skills.

When you take your car to a repair shop, you have certain expectations:

- You want it fixed right the first time.
- You want it fixed quickly. You don't want it out of service for a long time.

- You want it fixed soon. You want to have the repair work started soon after the problem is recognized.
- You want it repaired inexpensively. You don't mind paying a fair price for parts and labor, but you object to high mark-ups on parts and paying for people who are unproductive.

Now think about how an operator's involvement in maintenance compares to the way you deal with your own car. Most areas are much the same. If you are mechanically gifted, you may perform an unusual amount of maintenance and repairs, but mostly you leave tasks requiring special skills and tools to people who have them.

Generally speaking, it is best to use operators to perform tasks where they add equal or greater value than they would if they were focusing solely on operating the plant as well as it can be operated. As mentioned above, operators do not have "free time". They may have poorly-supervised time, but all their time is valuable and should be used and managed in a manner that provides the greatest benefit.

Operators' Role in the Routine Maintenance Process (RMP)

There are several tasks the operator must perform that are part of the RMP. If these tasks are performed poorly, the result will be lost effectiveness and efficiency, not only for themselves but for the entire maintenance effort. If the tasks are performed well, the positive results will leverage the value of the time spent by the operator.
- The operator must clearly describe requirements in

work requests. If requirements are well defined, work will be done right the first time.

- The operator must avoid writing unnecessary work orders. Some years ago a study showed that 80% of all work orders for instrument repairs were unnecessary. The operator had all the "time, talent, and tools" needed to take corrective action himself.
- The operator must see that equipment is prepared and work permits are ready for maintenance personnel to start on-time.
- Permits need to be issued in a timely manner and the operator must clearly explain any hazards associated with a job.
- The operator must sign off completed work in a timely manner and ensure that the job is complete, including clean up.

Operators' Role in the Turnaround Process (TAP)

Many of the same tasks performed by an operator as a part of the RMP are also required as successful contributions to the TAP. There is one significant difference. Far fewer of the craftspeople involved in a turnaround know their way around or understand the hazards in a plant. So, in the TAP, add the following task to the ones listed above for the RMP:

Provide plant knowledge and expertise to facilitate work

done by miscellaneous work crews during turnarounds.

Operators' Role in the Reliability Process

The area of reliability is the one area where an operator can add the greatest value to Maintenance Excellence. By understanding how equipment works, and knowing what actions are likely to cause damage or deterioration, the operator can take steps that will minimize the need for maintenance work.

In addition to "doing no harm" the operator is in a singularly good position to identify deterioration and to intervene before a failure can occur. The operator is (or should be) in intimate contact with all the equipment in a plant at frequent intervals, 24 hours per day, 7 days per week. Awareness of normal conditions and sensitivity to changes in conditions are the best tools an operator can offer in preventing deterioration from progressing to failure.

When performing Reliability Centered Maintenance (RCM) analysis, the recommendations can better be described in the form of objectives rather than specific tasks that are suited only to a specific craft. This approach makes it possible to identify a range of techniques that are available to fulfill the objectives. With many jobs, an objective can be met using a technique that has been simplified so that an operator can perform it as a part of his normal rounds. If the job is not part of his rounds, the task can be developed as an occasional job that is done during slow periods like evenings and weekends.

Let's use an example of several "craft jobs" that were simplified and turned into an objective that could be achieved by an operator.

Several years ago while performing an RCM analysis at a chemical plant, work on a sump that collected drainage from the plant was being discussed. All drainage from the plant had to be collected and treated for possible contamination. The sump had a primary pump and a spare. The primary pump was motor driven and the spare was driven by a steam turbine. Both pumps had tandem mechanical seals with a seal flush between the seals. The operation of the sump was as follows:

- At the low level, both pumps would be shut down.
- As the level of fluid in the sump increased, a valve opened to provide seal flush to the electrically-driven primary pump.
- At a slightly higher level, the electric pump started.
- If the level continued to increase, a small valve opened providing warm-up steam to the steam turbine.
- As the level continued to build, the valve providing seal flush to the steam- powered back up pump would open.
- If the level continued to build, the large steam valve would open, starting the steam-driven pump.
- If the level continued to increase, a local alarm, and an alarm in the control room, would sound.
- As flow into the sump came under control, all these devices would shut down in reverse order of start up.

While discussing this operation during the RCM analysis,

it became apparent that the operations personnel knew very little about how the sump worked, despite the fact that it had been in existence for many years and it was critical to environmental performance of the unit. At that time, a set of PM tasks was being performed by machinists, electricians, and instrument technicians, to ensure that all the systems described above worked properly. All the operator did was to prepare work permits and sign off the work as being completed. With the number of individual tasks being done, that work occupied a significant amount of time.

These tasks were revised to have the operator drag a fire hose over to the sump once a month. Using fire water, the operator filled the sump. At each distinct step, the operator verified that the proper action took place. If it did not, the operator would write a work request to have repairs done.

Switching from the earlier craft-based tasks to this service test, not only met the objectives but it also did the following:

1. Reduced maintenance costs for the crafts that had been involved.
2. Increased operator understanding of how the sump worked.
3. Eliminated a redundant task for inspecting the fire hose.
4. Maintained the same serviceability of the sump.

As compared with demolishing old piping or changing steam traps, this change to an operator task actually leveraged the value of the operator. Throughout a plant, there are a myriad of tasks that, when properly defined by true objectives and simplified, can improve plant reliability and support Maintenance Excellence.

My version of ORM is one that is based on simple concepts like the ones exemplified above.

Additional Thoughts from References

Wireman, Terry; *Inspection and Training for TPM;* Industrial Press, New York; 1992

There are a number of sources for thoughts on various approaches to Total Productive Maintenance. The reference cited above is particularly useful in that does not limit the reader to much of the "ritualistic" approach described in other books. As discussed in this chapter, I believe that the operator has a critical role in maintenance, but that role needs to be consistent with the culture where the plant or shop is located.

In my experience, one of the most difficult aspects of "operator-involved" maintenance programs is populating the comprehensive program of tasks that operators will be expected to perform. As described in the chapter on RCM, it is possible to identify the "what" by performing the RCM analysis in a manner that produces simplified tasks that can be performed by operators. The text that is referenced here is very useful in identifying the "how" for those tasks. Many operator-based activities are inspections. Operators can perform those tasks as well as anyone, if they know what to look for. The referenced text is useful in providing that knowledge.

CHAPTER 14
MAINTENANCE MEASURES

The greatest danger for most of us is not that our aim is too high and we miss it, but that it is too low and we reach it.

Michelangelo

The objective of creating and monitoring measures is to drive results. When you:

- Monitor a specific measure
- Show interest by asking for details and clarifications
- Provide input on desired results

It is a clear method of providing direction leading to specific results. A complete, accurate, and well-defined set of measures is a critical tool in achieving alignment between requirements and performance.

Hierarchy of Measures

It is not unusual to have some amount of misunderstanding in the various forms of measures used to characterize performance. It is important to understand how measures fit with one another because they need to be aligned, and they need to be assigned to individuals who have the authority and resources to achieve them.

At the top of the hierarchy of measures is the Strategic Plan that is being pursued. Positive results in each of the measures below the Strategic Plan should help ensure successful completion of the Strategic Plan.

Immediately below the Strategic Plan are Critical Success Factors. A Critical Success Factor is a measure that describes the "bottom line" performance for an organization. A Critical Success Factor cannot be directly controlled but results from the cumulative effects of Key Measures.

Below Critical Success Factors are Key Measures. A Key Measure is a factor that directly contributes to variation or change in Critical Success Factors. Most often, Key Measures are lagging indicators.

At the lowest level is the Process Measure. A Process Measure is a factor that contributes to change or variation in Key Measures, but is directly related to the process being used. When properly defined, Process Measures are leading indicators.

The Maintenance Measures we want to emphasize in this chapter are Process Measures. But, more specifically, they are Process Measures associated with the work management processes, like the RMP, that this book has highlighted as a part of a Strategic Plan for achieving

Maintenance Excellence. As mentioned earlier, all the measures have to be aligned from Strategic Plan to the tasks being performed every day in the field, to achieve the desired level of success.

The following chart helps describe the relationship between each of the levels described above:

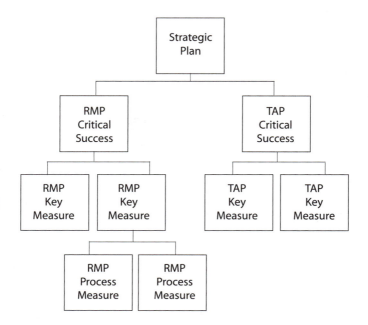

A simple example might help to explain the levels described on the next page.

In professional football, the strategic plan is to win the Super Bowl.

While that is the objective for all the NFL teams, it is also something over which they have very little direct control.

The Critical Success Factor that is helpful in determining how well a team is doing in moving toward achieving their objective is the number of games won in a season. It is possible for a team to win the Super Bowl while winning fewer games than another team, but it is clear that the team that wins the most games in each division will make the playoffs and have either a bye or home field advantage or both. Both those things provide a competitive advantage and make it more likely that the team will achieve its objective.

Key Measures are useful in determining how well a team has done in the past and by inference, how likely they are to perform well in the future. In football, some of the Key Measures are:

- Total Offense – Average total yards gained per game
- Total Defense – Average total yards given up to opposing teams per game
- Scoring Offense – Average points scored per game
- Scoring Defense – Average points given up to opposing teams per game

Again, these factors are not directly controllable, but they are more closely related to controllable factors than are Critical Success Factors (wins and losses). Also, although it is possible to forecast that a strong offensive team is likely to do well against a weak defensive team (and vice versa), this likelihood does not bear directly on the results of any specific game, or on achieving the over-all objective. If a strong offense fumbles the ball a number of times in any game, it can still lose to any opponent. Therefore, in addition to not being directly controllable, Critical Success Factors do not directly control success. But, they do provide a strong indicator of the likelihood of success.

Process measures or process indicators are the lowest level factor in this hierarchy. They are also the most controllable.

In football, there are two kinds of process indicator: individual and team.

From the individual perspective, a player can set the stage for success by working on his speed, strength and endurance. Direct measures that have been found to be useful in the past are:

- Percent body fat
- Time in the 60-yard dash
- Weight in the bench press
- Condition at the end of the fourth quarter

From a team perspective, the coaches can set the stage for success by working on knowledge and execution of plays and by selecting the appropriate process (form of offense and defense). Some of the direct measures that are useful include:

- Passing efficiency
- Blocking and Tackling effectiveness
- Kicking distance and accuracy
- Play selection and mix

In this example, as with Maintenance Excellence, it is not only important that the players play hard and well, it is also important to select the proper process. For example, many teams have been successful using some version of the so-called "West Coast Offense" because of its flexibility.

In the example, football, the ultimate measure of success, winning the Super Bowl, is a long way from the basic controllable factors: sound blocking and tackling, intelligent play selection, and individual conditioning. On the other hand, you will not get to the Super Bowl without the basics.

The same is true in Maintenance Excellence. Being the most reliable and the lowest cost producer is a long way from good planning, tight scheduling, managing break-ins, and sound estimating.

In either activity, it is impossible to be successful in achieving the strategic objective without first focusing on the basics. Our efficiency and effectiveness in the basics needs to be thoroughly measured by our process measures.

Achieving Strategic Objectives Using Maintenance Measures

Our strategic objective in Maintenance Excellence should be to become the low-cost producer.

There are two elements or Critical Success Factors associated with achieving this strategy:

1. Driving down costs
2. Driving up production

The maintenance function in a plant makes its contribution to driving down costs by completing the required maintenance as effectively and efficiently as possible. That effort translates to making the RMP and TAP work as well as possible.

The maintenance function makes its contribution to driving up production by increasing plant reliability and availability. That effort translates to making the Reliability Process work as well as possible.

For the RMP, the following are several of the Key Measures:

1. Craft productivity
2. Percent overtime
3. Workforce size

As mentioned earlier, these factors are not directly controllable. And if you try to control them without first controlling the underlying measures, you are headed for trouble. The size of the workforce and the amount of overtime should reflect the number of people needed to keep the plant operating reliably, not the number you can afford. For the RMP, the following are Process Measures:

- Work Input Rate in man-hours (how much work is being identified each day)
- Work Output Rate in man-hours (how much work is being completed by the current crew each day)

- Workable Backlog in weeks by craft (how much work is planned and ready to schedule)
- Estimating accuracy
- Schedule Attainment (portion of jobs completed as scheduled – a measure of the maintenance foreman's performance)
- Schedule Adherence (portion of jobs that are started as scheduled – a measure of the operations – maintenance coordinators performance)
- Number of Break-ins each day – (a measure of operations managements performance)

There are other Key Measures and Process Measures for the RMP, and my objective here is to show how they fit together.

I cannot control Craft Productivity directly, but I can control Schedule Attainment and Schedule Adherence directly. Since Schedule Attainment and Schedule Adherence have a direct impact on productivity, I manage productivity by addressing problems in those areas immediately, when there are problems.

For instance, if equipment is not ready, or permits are not ready on time for first job starts, the schedule will be disrupted and your productivity will suffer. To improve productivity, get first-starts back on schedule.

For the TAP, the following are several of the Key

Measures:

- P/A (planned man-hours versus man-hours consumed to achieve a specific point on the schedule)
- Schedule Performance (current status compared to expected status at this time)
- Budget Performance (current spending compared to expected spending at this point)

As discussed above, it is impossible to directly control these Key measures. But it is possible to control Process Measures that will directly affect these measures. For instance, you can address:

- Starting time (the time workers actually arrive at the job site and start work)
- Quitting time (the time workers actually stop working
- Length of breaks
- Time spent in travel
- Amount of unapproved work that is being done
- Amount of work that is outside the turnaround premises being done

All these measures are directly measurable and control-lable. Like blocking and tackling in football, they do not directly win Super Bowls, but they set the stage for the ability to win the Super Bowl.

For the Reliability Process, the following are a few of the Key Measures:

- Average Mean Time Between Failure (MTBF) of pumps and other equipment types

- Average Mean Time To Repair (MTTR) of pumps and other equipment types
- System Availability
- System Reliability
- CoUR (Cost of Un Reliability)

As with the RMP and TMP, Key Measures for reliability can not be controlled directly. Instead, they are the result of activities than can be measured using Process Measures.

For example, system reliability is the instantaneous likelihood that a system will fail during a specific period of time. The overall system reliability is the cumulative result of a number of other factors. For example:

- The inherent reliability of the system, as determined by the robustness of components of the system and the configuration (including redundancy) of the system
- The adequacy of the regimen of the program of predictive and preventive maintenance in achieving the system inherent reliability
- The discipline exercised in keeping up with the prescribed program of predictive and preventive maintenance
- The quality of repairs and overhaul maintenance conducted

A set of Process Measures that would be useful in ensuring that the "blocking and tackling" needed to achieve reliability would include the following:

- Percent of pro-active maintenance (number of pro-

active man-hours compared to reactive man-hours)
- Pro-active maintenance compliance (percentage of scheduled pro-active man-hours that are completed)
- Actual system reliability compared to predicted system reliability (the reliability being achieved compared to the reliability forecast using a mathematical simulation)
- Actual component reliability compared to predicted component reliability (the reliability being achieved for each critical component compared to the reliability forecast using a mathematical simulation)

Clearly, the last two measures are used as ways to "trick" the reader into performing reliability analysis on the entire system and individual components. Once you perform this analysis, you will learn three things:

1. Which parts of the system are "reliability limiters"?
2. Which components are not performing as advertised or simulated in my system model?
3. Is my pro-active maintenance program (predictive and preventive maintenance) delivering the full inherent reliability available from my system?

The real secret is to have a set of measures that drive response. If you know your reliability limiters, you can take action to make them more redundant or you can provide redundancy in your system to counteract their weakness. Once you know if your systems are achieving the full inherent reliability, you will know if there is any benefit to performing more pro-active maintenance or if you are achieving all "you have a right to expect". If current PM programs are delivering the full inherent reliability, more PM is a waste of time and money.

In concluding this chapter, I want to add that I have no intention to provide a long laundry list of measures. I have several such lists but I consider them counter-productive for a number of reasons.

1. Measurements are costly. They cost money to produce and distribute. They cost money to review. Responding to them costs time and money.
2. Most long lists of measures are measures of lagging indicators and you can do nothing to improve them. (The horse has already left the barn.)
3. Many measures in long lists have nothing to do with your strategic objectives. They are viewed as being "directionally correct".
4. The longer the list, the less likely that any one of them will cause action. The presence of unimportant measures tends to dilute the attention paid to important measures.

As a result, I recommend that you develop your own list of measures following the path described in this chapter.

- Start by identifying your Strategic Objectives.
- Based on your Strategic Objectives, identify the Critical Success Factors you believe will deliver those objectives.
- Identify the Key measures that tend to indicate if you

are achieving your Critical Success Factors.
- Finish by creating the sets of Process Measures that are designed to drive the individuals performing the key steps of your work management processes in the proper direction.

Additional Thoughts from References

Womack, James P. and Jones, Daniel T., *Lean Thinking,* Simon & Schuster, New York, 1996

Many canned lists of maintenance measures are aimed purely at identifying the current status of specific elements. For instance, "How much overtime is being used?" On the other hand, those measures provide no indication of the amount of waste that is occurring. For maintenance measures to be truly comprehensive, they must provide managers with some idea of the amount of waste that is occurring and where. The referenced text will be useful to the reader in deciding where best to look for waste and how to measure it to drive response.

Senge, Peter M.; *The Fifth Discipline, The Art & Practice of the Learning Organization;* Doubleday Publishing; New York; 1990

As with the last reference, when maintenance measures focus on the current status of a specific element, they do not support learning. Instead, they support reaction. Effective measures will provide feedback on the effect of responses. For instance, if I respond by closing the hot water valve a half turn, the water will become too cold. If I have a system for not only noting current status but recalling the change that led to that status, I can learn how much I should respond next time. The same is true of adjusting the size of your workforce. If your changes are always swinging between too many and too few, it is time to provide a feedback loop for learning in your process, so that you can quickly move to the proper workforce size.

APPENDIX:

Work Scoping Form - Page 1

Work Request #							Date:		
	Operator	Craft	Crew Size	Crew Hours	Special Skills		Craft		Total Hours
Pre Work						BM	Boilermaker		
Scaffold						CA	Carpenter		
Insulation						EL	Electrician		
Blinding						IN	Instrument		
Elect. Isolation						IS	Insulator		
Lighting						LA	Laborer		
Excavation						MA	Machinist		
Other						MR	Milwright		
Other						PA	Painter		
Other						PF	Pipefitter		
						OT	Other		
Main Activity							Total		
On-Site Work						**Special Requirements**			Y/N
						1. Breathing Air			
						2. Safety Equipment			
						a.			
						b.			
						c.			
Off-Site Work						3. Mobile/Lifting Equipment			
						a.			
						b.			
						c.			
Shop Work						4. Special Permits			
						a. Entry			
						b. Fire			
						c. Hole Watch			
Other						d. Fire Watch			
						e. Other			
						5. Services			
						a. X-ray			
Post Work						b. Inspection			
Scaffold						c. Hydroblast			
De-Blind						d. Other			
Paint						e. Other			
Insulate						6.Parts/Materials			
Energize Electrical						a.			
Test						b.			
Clean-Up						c.			
Other						d.			
Other						e.			
Comments:						f.			

Form 1. Work Scoping Form

Work Scoping Form - Page 2 - Equipment Requirements

Forklift:	Large	Medium	Small		

Crane:	15 Ton	30 Ton	50 Ton	100 Ton	200 Ton

Truck:	P/U	Boomtrk	Staketrk	Flatbed	

Breathing Air:	SCBA	Cartridge	Dust		

PPE	Chemsuit	Greengear	Hotsuit		

Sketch / Comments:

Form 2 – Work Scoping Form

REFERENCES FOR FURTHER READING:

1. Abernethy, Dr. Robert B.; *The New Weibull Handbook – Fifth Edition*; Robert B. Abernethy, North Palm Beach, Florida; 2004

2. Conner, Daryl R., *Managing at the Speed of Change,* Villard Books, New York, 1992

3. Daley, Daniel T.; *The Little Black Book of Reliability Management*; Industrial Press, New York; 2007

4. Ireson, W. Grant & Coombs, Clyde F.& Moss, Richard Y. ; *Handbook of Reliability Engineering and Management – Second Edition;* McGraw-Hill, New York; 1996

5. Lamb, Richard G., *Availability Engineering & Management for Manufacturing Plant Performance,* Prentice-Hill Inc., New York, 1995

6. Latino, Robert J. & Latino, Kenneth C. ; *Root Cause Analysis – Improving Performance for Bottom Line Results*; CRC Press, New York; 1999

7. Levitt, Joel; *Managing Maintenance Shutdowns*

and Outages; Industrial Press, New York, 2004

8. Lewis, James P.; *Fundamentals of Project Management, Second Edition;* AMACOM, New York; 2001

9. Nyman, Don and Levitt, Joel; *Maintenance Planning, Scheduling and Coordination;* Industrial Press, New York; 2001

10. O'Connor, Patrick D. T. ; *Practical Reliability Engineering – Fourth Edition;* John Wiley & Sons, LTD; West Sussex, England; 2002

11. Senge, Peter M.; *The Fifth Discipline, The Art & Practice of the Learning Organization;* Doubleday Publishing; New York; 1990

12. Smith, Anthony M., *Reliability Centered Maintenance,* McGraw-Hill Inc., New York, 1993

13. Thomsett,.Michael C. ; *The Little Black Book of Project Management;* AMACOM, New York; 1990

14. Wireman, Terry; *Computerized Maintenance Management Systems*; Industrial Press, New York; 1994

15. Wireman, Terry; *Inspection and Training for TPM*; Industrial Press, New York; 1992

16. Wireman, Terry; *World Class Maintenance Management*; Industrial Press, New York; 1990

17. Womack, James P. and Jones, Daniel T., *Lean Thinking,* Simon & Schuster, New York, 1996

INDEX